Business Writing

for

Busy People

By
Philip R. Theibert

CAREER PRESS
3 Tice Road
P.O. Box 687
Franklin Lakes, NJ 07417
1-800-CAREER-1
201-848-0310 (NJ and outside U.S.)
FAX: 201-848-1727

BUSINESS WRITING FOR BUSY PEOPLE
ISBN 1-56414-223-X, $15.99
Cover design by The Visual Group
Cover photo by Andrew Sacks/Tony Stone Images
Printed in the U.S.A. by Book-mart Press

To order this title by mail, please include price as noted above, $2.50 handling per order, and $1.00 for each book ordered. Send to: Career Press, Inc., 3 Tice Road, P.O. Box 687, Franklin Lakes, NJ 07417.

Or call toll-free 1-800-CAREER-1 (NJ and Canada: 201-848-0310) to order using VISA or MasterCard, or for further information on books from Career Press.

Library of Congress Cataloging-in-Publication Data

Theibert, Philip R.
    Business writing for busy people / by Philip R. Theibert.
        p.   cm.
    Includes index.
    ISBN 1-56414-223-X (pbk.)
    1. Business writing. 2. English language--Business English.
    I. Title.
    HF5718.3.T48   1996
    808'.06665--dc20   95-52633
                                                               CIP

Dedication

To Kathleen, who has been there every step of the way.

Acknowledgments

When you finish a book, you realize you owe a lot of people a big thank-you. This book has been edited by many fine editors. The first editor, when it was merely a collection of loose-leaf pages, was Nelle Thorne, a retired elementary librarian who knows her stuff and can still teach us "youngsters" a thing or two about grammar and syntax.

This book also greatly benefited from the capable editing of Debra Hart May who with a light hand and good humor made this a much better book. I must also thank Ellen Scher, associate editor, who deciphered the comments I scrawled on the manuscript with a fountain pen.

Of course, a special thanks must go to Ron Fry, who first believed in this project and helped shepherd it through to fruition.

Not to be forgotten are the many professionals around the country who attended my writing seminars and helped contribute their ideas and suggestions. Some even contributed corporate memos and reports; some were so bad, we all cringed.

Finally, a special thanks to "famous" Claire and Tebby, my children who put up with a father demanding they "keep the noise down" so he could work. I also owe thanks to my wife Kathleen, but I'm not sure if a mere thank-you is enough to pay off that debt! One can only hope.

Contents

Preface

This is a very eclectic book on business writing. It contains poems from e.e. cummings, letters from Charles Dickens and essays from E.B. White among many other pieces. Yet, as eclectic as some of these selections may be, there is a fine madness behind this book. Good writing is more than just properly lining up all the subjects, verbs, pronouns and prepositions in a row. It involves a feeling for words and a willingness to show, at times, a playful spirit and, at other times, a serious spirit.

The purpose of this book is to go beyond the standard book on "how to write properly." The purpose of this book to put a little soul into your writing so someone knows that it comes from you, a real human being, and not some robot sitting in Cubicle #17. God knows, business writers could use a little more soul, a little more warmth, a little more humanity to replace the endless string of clichés and gibberish that too often masquerade as "proper writing."

But above all, I hope this book teaches you how important writing is to your career. As I emphasize in the introduction, how you write reflects how you think. Before we move on, let me share a quick story with you that illustrates this point. A friend of mine was interviewing a CEO for a speech he was writing for him. When the interview was over the CEO walked over to his desk, pulled a file from his drawer and laid it on his desk. He said, "This company has more than 8,000 employees. There is no way I can keep track of the thinking ability of each employee. But I can keep track of the letters, memos and reports that cross my desk. I keep the well-written ones that show thoughtfulness and insight in this file. These letters, memos and reports show me these people have the ability to think and communicate. I have my top officers keep an eye on these people. After a certain point, everyone has acquired the same technical skills. Those who can communicate well are the ones we'll promote. That's why this file is so valuable. These are my excellent communicators, the future leaders in this company."

Remember this story as you struggle to become a better writer. It's well worth the effort and energy.

So here's to making you a better writer. Carry this book with you, thumb through it, enjoy it!

Introduction

I have traveled extensively around the country presenting writing seminars to executives. I ask them why they're taking the writing seminar, and I get the same standard response.

"Communication skills are the number one reason people get promoted."

They're right, but they are missing an even more important reason. You don't take a writing class or read a book like this merely to get promoted. You take a writing class also to help develop your thinking skills.

I have spent many years writing speeches for CEOs. And when we're relaxing, after I have taped their thoughts for the speech, we often get on the subject of writing. And time after time CEOs tell me that the best way to determine an employee's thinking ability is to check his or her writing.

If the writing is muddled, if it wanders, if it has no logical order, if it is hastily thrown together with no attention to details, if it makes basic grammar mistakes, if the style is stiff and wooden, following a simple subject-verb, subject-verb pattern, that CEO has discovered a lot about that employee. And it's all there on a single piece of paper.

Top executives also understand that when you leave a client, part of you stays behind for that client to examine in detail. That part is whatever piece of writing you have left with him or her.

CEOs also know another basic fact. If you don't have time to write, you don't have time to think. Sure, that's the same line your fifth-grade teacher handed you, but you know what? She was right.

Good writing is time-consuming because it forces you to think. All of those thoughts and ideas, beliefs and opinions floating around in your head have to be actually marshaled, put under control and expressed clearly and logically on paper.

Is that easy? No. Even starting an outline and trying to wedge your vague thoughts into some sort of logical sequence is tough. Putting your words on paper gets even tougher as you try to capture what you hope is the essence of an exquisite thought process. Put your thoughts on paper, and there they are staring back at you. If they *sound* stupid, that's a clue—they may actually *be* stupid.

In addition, when you put your thoughts on paper, people actually expect you to back them up. And then you must spend even more time reading and researching to see if your thoughts really do jibe with the facts.

The simple truth is that good thinking, which takes a lot of time and research, translates into good writing. Again, top executives know this.

To put it in its starkest terms, you should worry about what you write. This may be unfair, but people do judge you by how you write. A slight mistake here, a detail left out there, an overall lack of research—all build a case against you. And every mistake you make in a piece of writing plants a tiny bit of suspicion in your client's or boss's mind. They see the mistakes as chinks in your armor.

Is that fair? No.

But the good news—yes, there is finally good news—is that I have gathered up writing tips collected from my more than 20 years of writing experience and have placed them in this book.

My 20 years of writing experience includes extensive experience as a newspaper reporter, magazine editor, advertising copywriter, corporate speechwriter and author of four books and more than 500 magazine articles. In every writing job I have had, I have listened and taken extensive notes. This book represents the culmination of those years of experience, gathered for you in one easy-to-read volume.

Read these tips carefully, do the exercises, and I guarantee you will become a much better writer!

So let's get started.

Three main reasons to write

- The written word, be it in a memo, letter or report, still remains one of the best ways to showcase ideas, to understand each other, to inform (or misinform), to persuade and to urge action.

- You can never escape words, the very substance of writing. You even think in words. If your language is muddled, your thinking may be too.

- People judge you and you reveal yourself through what you write, the way you handle the written word. "Has he written anything?" Napoleon asked about a candidate, "Let me see his style."

1

Organization:
the key to success

"If you don't know where you're going, you could wind up somewhere else."

—Yogi Berra

Remember when you were in school taking essay tests? The teacher always told you to write an outline in the margins first. It didn't have to be a fancy outline, just a list of the key ideas you wanted to cover.

This gave your essay a sense of direction. It helped you to see where you were headed and what point or conclusion you wanted to reach; it helped you to support the main points.

I cannot state it often enough: *Always write an outline before you write anything else*. I am amazed at the number of people who just jump right in, and halfway through the letter, report or presentation, they realize it is not going well at all. They've made too many side trips, neglected too many important points that should have been made early, and soon reach the conclusion with the audience unsure of what trip they've been on, how they got there and why they should take the time and effort to read anything else the person writes.

If you are organized, if you have your main points, your thoughts, your back-up examples all lined up before you write, you have won half the battle. You are starting on a journey and you know where you are headed.

3

The following sections will help you organize your thoughts and writing. A little preparation up front will save you a lot of grief down the line!

Look at it this way. If you don't outline first, if you don't line up your ideas, *you are diving off the board then hoping to put water into the pool.*

Ask the right question!

Isidor I. Rabi, a Nobel Laureate in physics, was once asked, "Why did you become a scientist rather than a doctor or lawyer or businessman like the other immigrant kids in your neighborhood?"

His answer should be engraved in your mind before you start writing anything. He said, "My mother made me a scientist without ever intending it. Every other Jewish mother in Brooklyn would ask her child after school, 'So, did you learn anything today?' But not my mother. She always asked me a different question. 'Izzy,' she would say, 'Did you ask a good question today?' That difference, asking good questions, made me become a scientist."

Before writing anything (even an outline), make sure you're asking the right question. You could ask the wrong question and write an entire report on why buggy whip sales are decreasing, when the real question is "Why are we in the buggy whip business?"

Make sure you are asking and answering the most important questions, not the ones that people mistakenly believe are important.

For example, let's say you are writing a report—at the turn of the century—for a buggy whip manufacturer. He wants you to describe the market for some investors. The first question you ask is, "What will the market be like?" The answer is, "Terrible." The word "terrible" gives you a brief report, but won't help your boss or the investors.

The next question you ask is, "How do we succeed in a dwindling market?" This question puts us a little closer to the reality of the situation. And by exploring and writing about "how to succeed in a dwindling market," you have presented a report to your boss and investors they can really use. By presenting options for success, you have started to steer the report and the company in the right direction. And it all started by asking the right questions.

One way to know if you're asking and answering the most important questions is to get outside opinions. Ask your customers, ask the pros who track and analyze your industry, ask anyone associated with your company—including vendors. They will give you a perspective you don't get by asking insiders and they will help guide you to the proper questions that need to be asked and answered.

Consider this: if an organization or business is headed in the wrong direction, the last thing it needs to do is get there more efficiently. The same thought applies to any piece of writing. Make sure you're headed in the right direction before you begin to write.

Clarify what your boss wants up front

Many people tell me they are afraid to write because they are sure that their boss will say, "That's not what I wanted!" They say they have written a letter, memo or even a report for their boss and it has come back, bleeding with red ink—corrections and harsh criticism.

How can you avoid writing the wrong thing? Again, a lot of trouble can be avoided up front, before you even begin to write, with the right organizational techniques.

Perhaps the most basic organizational technique is this: Get agreement up front on what your boss wants you to write!

How do you avoid this? How do you get agreement up front? It's very simple. Ask questions. "What do you want this letter or report to cover?" "How long do you want it?" "What specific areas do we need to discuss?"

And of course, take extensive notes. Then—and this is a very important part of the process—about an hour later, send your boss a short note, with bullet points. The note might look like this:

> *Boss:*
> *Just to make sure we're on the same wavelength.*
> *The report will:*
> * *Be approximately four pages.*
> * *Discuss our latest venture into the travel market.*
> * *Give specific sales results so far.*
> * *Conclude with an estimate of June's sales results.*

Notice this memo is not more than seven lines long. Sometimes it might be longer. But if the boss sees this before you begin to write anything, believe me, you have saved yourself a lot of trouble.

A pep talk before we begin

You cannot start any writing project with a sense of insecurity. You must have confidence in yourself. Just like a hitter in baseball, if you begin by thinking you are going to fail, the odds are you will. The good hitters in baseball step up to the plate with a strong sense of confidence. You must have that same sense of confidence when you write.

Of course, the best way to get that sense of confidence is to over-prepare and over-research. You must have your subject matter down cold. The "tip of the iceberg" theory especially applies to writing. When your reader sees a report you wrote, he or she sees only the tip of the iceberg, not the mountains of research hidden beneath the sea that the tip is founded upon.

Most writers I know are overwhelmed at the amount of work they must do for a report. Again, don't panic. As the writer Ann LaMott points out, take it "bird by bird." She explains how her brother had a major report due on birds. He had photos of birds and facts about birds spread all over his desk. He felt overwhelmed. Finally, his father came by, patted him on the shoulder and said, "Son, just take it bird by bird."

Also, don't be crushed if not everyone loves your writing style. Remember: "Man has no greater urge than to change another man's copy." And if your copy always seems to be returned with red marks on it, if it looks like someone bled all over it, again, don't panic. Simply remember that in many corporate structures, people have to justify their positions. And sometimes the easiest way to do that is to write all over your report even if their ideas are bad. That proves they have read it and made their suggestions; they have done "their job."

And remember this: Even with the best of intentions and the best preparations, some days it ain't gonna be there! Everyone hits a slump, even writers. Give yourself a break, take a walk around the block, come back to it the next morning. Don't beat yourself up over it.

And if you fail—beware, I told you we were taking an eclectic approach to business writing—remember these famous people who failed:

- R.H. Macy failed seven times before his store in New York caught on.
- John Creasey, English novelist, got 753 rejection slips before he published 564 books.
- Babe Ruth struck out 1,330 times, but he also hit 714 home runs.
- Abraham Lincoln's track record:

  1832 - failed in business

  1832 - failed in bid for Illinois House of Representatives

  1855 - failed in bid for senate seat

  1856 - failed in bid for vice-president

And remember Walter Chrysler

You are not going to write perfectly the first time around. Many products benefit by being closely examined, taken apart, then reassembled— to determine how they can be made better.

In fact, one of my favorite stories involves Walter Chrysler. He saved his small pay as a railroad mechanic to buy a huge $5,000 Pierce-Arrow sedan—just to take it apart, put it together again, and see what he could see. He wanted to find a way to make a better car and went at it by asking himself specific questions such as, "Why wouldn't brakes on all four wheels stop the car even better?" "Why not keep the lubricating oil in better condition by having it run through a filter at all times?" "Wouldn't tires of a bigger diameter give a smoother ride?"

Needless to say, none of us drives a Pierce-Arrow today, but many of us drive a Chrysler. The same theory Chrysler applied to engineering a new car should apply to engineering your writing. Don't be afraid to take it apart, look at it and keep coming up with new ideas to make it better.

Plus, the best way to learn how to organize a report or letter is to take a stack of reports and letters you like and, just like Walter Chrysler, take them apart and put them back together. See how the ideas flow. Look at the beginnings and endings. See what holds the middles together.

Louis L'Amour didn't start writing best-selling Westerns overnight. No, he taught himself how by taking a stack of the best-selling Westerns of the time and reading and re-reading them over and over. He studied them, just as Walter Chrysler studied that Pierce-Arrow.

Two more pieces of advice. The first is crucial. No matter how much confidence you have and no matter how good you are, no one writes a masterpiece the first time out. After you have finished what you think is a great report, put it on your desk and let it cool off overnight. Then come back the next morning and look at it.

In fact, this *Paris Review* interview with Ernest Hemingway shows how important rewriting can be.

Interviewer: *"How much rewriting do you do?"*

Hemingway: *"It depends. I rewrote the ending of* A Farewell to Arms, *the last page of it, 39 times before I was satisfied."*

Interviewer: *"Was there some technical problem there? What was it that had stumped you?"*

Hemingway: *"Getting the words right."*

The final bit of advice? Don't be afraid of writing. Just remember Bob Gibson's advice to other pitchers, "Bring all you got."

Know to whom you are writing: key questions to ask

Get a sense of your audience and yourself!

As Professor Harold Hill said in *The Music Man,* "You gotta know the territory." Before you begin any writing, you must have a good sense of what you want to accomplish, who your readers are and what actions you want them to take.

In short, you need to have these questions answered before you begin to write:

1. **Who are you as a writer?** In other words, are you writing as a manager, a friend, a consultant, an expert in some field? What is your voice?

2. **Who are your readers?** Are they management professionals, front-line employees, people you barely know, potential clients? Know who your readers are going to be so you can slant your writing to best suit their needs.

3. **What have you discovered through research or previous contact with the reader that will help you write this better?** You may be promoting a new product to a client. You may know that the price is not really what matters—he wants proof that it works. Then in this specific letter to this specific client, load the letter up with facts, figures, research, testimonials—anything that will give him an idea of the product's effectiveness.

4. **Do you know what the reader wants or needs?** If not, how will you find out before putting the wrong thing on paper?

5. **Why are you addressing the reader and on what subject?**

6. **What is your relationship to the subject matter?** Are you an expert on the subject? Are you seeking information on the subject?

7. **How do you want your reader to relate to the subject matter?**

8. **Why are you writing this?**

9. **What is your objective?**

10. **What key questions must you answer?** Every author knows about the MDQ. The major dramatic question. Every good story revolves around the MDQ. Will the kidnapped boy make it home safely? Will the two lovers finally find each other? Will the stolen diamonds be recovered? This same principle applies to anything you are writing. What are the major questions you must answer for your reader? Cost? Effectiveness of the product? Delivery of the product? Estimate of construction time? Before you start writing, write down the major questions your reader has and make sure you answer them.

11. **What objections, if any, do you anticipate the reader may have?**

12. **How are you going to persuade this reader that your service or your solution fits his or her needs?**

13. **What will your opening statement be?**

14. **How will you get a commitment for the next step?** Most memos, letters and reports are written for a reason. That reason might be to inform, to clarify an issue, to sell a product, to analyze two different approaches to a problem. Well, you get the idea. After the report, letter or memo is read, the reader is thinking, "Well, what am I expected to do about this? Am I supposed to take any steps, make any decisions? Or am I simply to sit and wait until she gets back to me?" Make sure that after you have written that great letter, memo or proposal, your reader not only knows *why* it was written, but also *what* he or she is expected to do about it.

How to present information: 10 key ways

Sitting down and starting to outline your memo, letter, proposal or report can be very frustrating. Figuring out how you should organize your facts, figures, events and other material is very difficult.

The list on pages 10 and 11 can help you get organized. Before you begin to outline, study this list and, chances are, you'll discover that your report falls into one of these formats. Knowing this helps tremendously;

once you have the format roughed out, putting your thoughts into outline form is much easier.

1. **Time sequence.** This format describes the time that events take place. For example, you are preparing to market a new product. You should describe the time schedule, beginning with the initial design stage, proceeding through the prototype stage, alpha, beta testing and so forth.

2. **Place.** This format almost reads like a map, going logically from one location to another. For example, you may be reporting sales figures in different parts of the country. You would go from west to east or east to west. So if you went west to east, you would report on sales in Los Angeles, Phoenix, Oklahoma City, etc.

3. **Chain of command.** This format looks like an organizational ladder. You are describing the people who will look at and analyze a report. Go from front-line worker to CEO or reverse the order. But don't start with a V.P., then go to a front-line worker, then back to the CEO.

4. **Procedure.** This format uses a logical sequence of steps. For example, your company is moving to a new office building. List the steps and the procedures in the order needed to complete the move successfully.

5. **Overview to specific.** This format takes you from a bird's eye view to specific details. Paint a broad picture of where your company wants to be in five years. Then list the steps needed to get there.

6. **Specific to overview.** This format takes you from the details to the overall picture. For example, you will add new salespeople, you will put more money into advertising, you will gain more retail outlets. These specific steps will give you a company selling 20,000 widgets a year within two years.

7. **Top priority to bottom priority.** This format lists the actions you must take, beginning with the most important action and ending with the least important action. Some people feel it is the best way to list action steps. Others feel it builds no suspense. If you begin with your most important step, will your audience or reader lose attention as each action you describe becomes less important?

8. **Bottom priority to top priority.** This format lists the most important action you must take at the end of your letter, memo, report or proposal. Proponents of this method think it build a sense of excitement, a sense of anticipation. Plus the most important step (the one listed last) is the one the readers will take away with them because that's the last thing they read. But a flaw with this approach is that you are betting the reader reads the whole letter and gets to the final, most important step.

9. **Cause to effect.** This format lists the cause of something, then tells the effect. For example, Jones fell asleep on the assembly line, thus the toy went past him without a safety check. Smith was out to lunch that day and there was a temp taking his place at quality control. The temp thought the toy was "okay." The effect of these two actions is that your company sold a defective toy.

10. **Effect to cause.** This format begins with the result of your actions. For example, your company is being besieged by angry consumers. That's the effect. The cause was that you dumped hazardous waste in a preschool playground. Start with effect, then move to cause.

The destination way of thinking

Think of any piece of writing as a destination. Your readers get on with you at Point A. They have a limited amount of knowledge. You want them to ride with you past at least three train stations. At each train station, they pick up a new bit of knowledge. Finally, when your readers get off the train, you shake their hands, give them a quick send-off speech about what they've learned, ask them for action and tell them you expect to see them soon.

Let's walk through this train station analogy. You are writing to an audience about a United Fund Raising Campaign. You know your readers get on at Point A with a vague sense that United Fund is a charity that helps people. At Station One you might introduce them to some of the people the agency helps. At Station Two you might introduce your readers to some people the agency would like to help but can't. At Station Three you might mention the funds needed to help these additional people.

Finally, at Station Four your readers are ready to get off the train. You thank them for their attention, repeat the information you have given them, reinforce what is needed to help more people, then send them off with a promise that you'll call them soon for their commitment to the United Fund drive.

On this short journey with you, your readers started off with limited knowledge. You gave them additional information at each station and then sent them off with an idea planted in their minds.

Write a simple sentence

Before you even begin to outline, write one simple sentence. That sentence is the crux of your whole letter, memo, proposal or report.

For example, that one line defining your document might read: *I want this company to quit photocopying everything in sight because it is costing us $10,000 a year in unnecessary expenses.*

Ask three basic questions

Now put down three questions on that same piece of paper. First **"What is this about?"** That's fairly simple. You've decided everyone is running around making too many darn copies.

The second question is **"Why should my reader be interested?"** Now this is where you must know your audience. If the reader is the big boss, obviously, he wants to save money. But what about the sales rep down the hall who thinks the copy machine was installed to copy Johnny's homework or to pass out office jokes to everyone in sight?

She doesn't care if the copies are costing the company five cents a shot. It's not her money. Unless, of course, you can convince her it is *her* money she's wasting. Perhaps it affects her bonus check? The point is that your argument for eliminating the unnecessary copies must consider everyone who will read it, anticipate his or her response and be prepared for it. You must have something planted in that letter that will show all potential readers **what's in it for them.**

The third question is **"What should my reader do about this?"** Okay, you're not talking rocket science here. Quit making copies! Of course it might help to be more specific. Quit making copies of your hand, your face, jokes, recipes—in short, if you can't justify copying it for work, please don't copy it!

No matter how big or complicated the writing project you're working on is, ask these three simple questions: **What is this about? Why should my reader be interested?** and **What should my reader do about it?** These questions should help guide you through most letters, memos and presentations.

Let's look at a short memo that would have benefited from this approach:

> *Judy, it seems there has been some confusion over parking garage arrangements. Before March you used to have your parking expenses deducted from your paycheck and paid by Sylabus Inc. Once you became an MQ employee, Joyce Beard said she informed you Sylabus would no longer be making the payment for your parking and requested you turn in your Sylabus card. When you were hired by MQ, your compensation modeled your previous package and did not include parking. Apparently, you continued to use a Sylabus parking card that they did not pay for anymore. This use has resulted in an outstanding bill for the past two months' use. Sylabus understands that you might be confused about how parking arrangements should have been made these past couple months but asks that you settle the balance with the garage and make arrangements to pay the garage directly in the future. If it would make paying less confusing, MQ would be willing to establish the same payroll deduction arrangement that you had with Sylabus.*

Wow! There's a memo. Yet, it can be easily fixed. Let's try our simple approach. First of all, let's write our simple sentence that states our main objective: We want Judy to pay her bill, quit using her old parking card and make new arrangements to pay for parking.

Question 1. What is this about?
Answer: Judy is using the wrong parking card and has run up a two-month bill.

Question 2. Why should my reader be interested?
Answer: If Judy keeps up this nonsense, someone will tow her car away.

Question 3. What should Judy do about this?
Answer: Pay her bill and make arrangements with the garage.

Now, watch how short and understandable we can make this memo when we use our new approach:

> *Judy, you have been using the wrong parking card. The one you have been using has been invalid for two months. Your former employer no longer pays parking. This has caused a problem. You owe the garage two months' rent. You must pay it or they will impound your car. After you pay your past rent, make arrangements with the garage to pay them directly every month. Or chat with me, and we can deduct it from your paycheck. Thanks.*

One reason the writer of the first Judy memo got into trouble was that he was trying to protect her feelings. He didn't want to come out and say, "Listen, you deadbeat. You've been using an invalid parking card and have been stiffing the garage. Pay up and make arrangements. Now!"

In a way he was right. That would have been too harsh a memo. But by tiptoeing around Judy's feelings, the writer caused another problem. Judy had to struggle through dense prose to figure out what he was driving at.

Make this a simple rule: People want to be treated like adults. Tell them the truth honestly and openly. Sure, use a little tact, but don't beat around the bush.

Go back and compare the first Judy memo to the second. Notice how much more straightforward the second is without hurting Judy's feelings. It's just telling her the truth in a way most adults would like to hear it.

The "because" approach

You're proposing a new idea to management. The idea can be anything, from outsourcing the payroll department to hiring more staff, from buying new equipment to changing office parks.

When you sell an idea to anyone, you have to convince them it's the right way to go. We've already touched on the best way to sell an idea in "Why should my reader be interested?"

Of course, coming up with reasons why they should care about your idea is not always easy. That's when you can start the *because* game. Sit down and start writing a bunch of clauses beginning with *because*. How absurd some of them sound doesn't matter. The point is that you want to line up your ammunition.

So if you're asking for more staff, your *because* list might look like this:

- Because too many people are working overtime.

- Because we need expertise in certain areas.

- Because I want to boss around a lot of people.

- Because more staff will improve our productivity.

- Because the cost of hiring these people will pay for itself through new clients.

- Because my wife would like to see me home before 8 p.m. every night.

- Because my staff is getting hostile, and I think they might lock me in the men's room.

Analyze the counter-arguments

A mistake many people make when they write a letter or report is failing to analyze the counter-arguments. As you did with the *Because* clauses, list the counter-arguments you can expect. Of course, you cannot and may not want to answer all the arguments in your letter or report, but identifying the most important counter-arguments right away is important.

For example, let's look again at adding more staff. Your boss might say:

- Sales are down.
- We can't afford the extra insurance it will cost us.
- It would be easier to contract the work out.
- You can't handle the workers you have now.
- You wouldn't need to pay overtime if you were more efficient.
- Your wife is sick of you anyway.

In short, to make your proposal as strong as possible, anticipate your reader's response and prepare for it.

The logical outline

Another way to approach organizing your material is through the logical outline. It looks like this:

Define your terms. Tell your audience what you're going to talk about and, if it's an abstract concept, explain it so you both feel comfortable with the concept. For example, if you're talking about strategic planning, you might want to include a brief description of what strategic planning is.

Also, remember that people may have different understandings of the same concept. I recall a time when my wife and I were camping, and we met a couple by the brook. My wife told them we were going across the country in a Honda. They were too. Halfway through the conversation, I realized that while my wife was talking about a Honda car, the couple was talking about a Honda motorcycle. The couple would say, "Doesn't the wind bother you?" And my wife would say, "Not at all." Then they would move on to another topic.

Well, my wife walked away thinking she had had a splendid conversation. When I pointed out that the others were talking about a Honda motorcycle, she didn't believe me at first.

True, both used the same term, "Honda," but by not defining the term up front, they thought they were communicating when they really weren't.

State the problem, its causes and effects. What may seem serious to you, such as not having enough staff to do the work, may seem trivial to your audience. In this section of the outline, you must clearly state the problem, the reason it exists and what will happen if nothing is done about it. In other words, you are saying to your readers, "This is why you must pay attention to this problem."

Weigh alternative solutions. This is the section in which you can show you're not just pushing your own agenda. You have given a lot of thought to this problem and are ready to consider all possible solutions. This section is a good chance to show your thinking power and how analytical you are.

Propose and analyze the solution you advocate. Now narrow down the report or letter to the best solution. Tell why it is the best solution and what advantages will be gained by accepting your proposal.

Discuss its implementation. Notice that you have not asked for their acceptance. You have made a strategic move here: You've assumed they agree with you that it is the best proposal. Now move ahead and give them the "good hands" feeling. Show them you are in control and you've even thought of the most efficient and easiest way to implement the plan.

The motivated sequence

This sequence is easy to remember. Just commit to memory these five words, in sequence: *attention, need, satisfaction, visualization, action.*
Here, in a bit more detail, is how this system works:

Get their attention. This is the sentence or paragraph of the letter, report or memo that grabs your readers' attention. You cannot be too shy. Sometimes the more dramatic the statement, the better. For example, don't say, "There has been a drastic decline in sales over the last three quarters." Be even more specific and dramatic. Say, "We have lost 20 customers and more than $1 million in sales; if the present trend continues, we will be in bankruptcy by next fall."

Show the need. In this section you show the need for your customers to buy a product, for your boss to give you 20 extra days of vacation or for your teenage son to start paying his own car insurance. For example, you might be selling a service that picks up rental videos. You tell your customers that they never return their videos on time, it's an extra hassle they don't need, and they always end up paying late charges for their kids' videos. There is a *need* here. They must do something about the problem of returning videos.

Satisfy the need. You have planted the need in your readers' minds. They understand there is a need. Now without wasting time, you show them the solution. Again, your customers have a problem returning those rental videos. Now, tell your customers how, for only $1, you'll return those videos for them.

Visualize the results or the benefits. Show your readers the benefits of your solution. Show them how that new car will gain them respect, how that new vacuum will give them time to paint the house on the weekends, how those extra people you hire will make the office a dream come true. Let's return to our video example. Paint a picture for your readers. Tell them how they won't wake up sweating at 3 a.m. with this terror that their child really has 20 videos hidden in that jungle she calls a room and you owe the video store $1,000. Why won't they have this nightmare? Because they have used your video return service. (Now if only there were a service for your kid's room!)

You really should paint a picture in the mind of your audience; have them visualizing the new life, the better life your solution will lead to.

Action. By now, you have given your audience a whole scenario. Like a good boxer, you have set them up. Now make your move.

Request action or approval at this point. Be specific. Don't say, "I'll wait for you to get back to me." Say, "You should buy this product this month because...." Create a desire for action; give them an urgent need to buy the product or approve the project. Returning one more time to our video return example, tell your potential customers they can have video peace of mind by calling your service right now and setting up an account. By doing so, they'll even receive a night's free video rental.

What are they going to do about it?

Perhaps this story about Thomas Carlyle, the nineteenth century Scottish philosopher, best sums up the "action segment" of your presentation. One Sunday morning Carlyle was getting dressed to deliver a speech to a large audience. His mother was sitting near the front door. She asked, "And where might you be going, Thomas?"

He replied, "Mother, I'm going to tell the people what's wrong with the world."

His mother tugged gently on his sleeve and said, "Yes, Thomas. But are you going to tell them what to do about it?"

That's what your action segment does. It tells people "what to do about it."

The seven key question technique

This technique is a close cousin to the motivated sequence. With it, you seemingly tap into your readers' minds and answer their key questions.

1. Exactly what is the nature of the problem?
2. How serious is it?
3. Are other people (besides me) affected?
4. Is an immediate action called for?
5. What courses of action are possible?
6. Which of these courses will produce the best solution?
7. Which solution will solve the problem quickly and at least cost and inconvenience?

Now let's look at an example of how we can use these questions. Your boss asks you to write a letter discussing the sales result of the previous quarter. Your company is employee-owned and all employees will receive the letter. You outline the letter by beginning with the first question and then move through the other questions. Your outline might look like this:

1. Exactly what is the nature of the problem?
   - Sales are down by 10 percent.
   - This represents a decline in revenue of $20,000.

2. How serious is it?
   - At this point, not that serious.
   - Sales of our sunscreen were affected by two months of unexpected rain on the East Coast.
   - Our previous quarter sales were 20 percent higher than we expected, so our cash flow is fine.

3. Are other people (besides me) affected?
   - Yes. Since is it an employee-owned company, we are all concerned when sales drop.
   - This letter is to inform you of the latest developments.

4. Is an immediate action called for?
   - Yes, because we should be prepared to take specific actions if the trend of decreasing sales continues.

5. What courses of action are possible?
   - We can offset falling sales in our sunscreen line by introducing new products.
   - We can be more aggressive in our advertising campaign.
   - We can offer discounts to our retailers.
   - We can search for more efficient ways of producing the product, thus giving us a higher profit margin.
   - We can examine all costs not directly related to manufacturing and selling our product and drastically reduce these costs.

6. Which of these courses will produce the best solution?
   - At this point, indicate to your readers that you are not sure which course of action should be taken, but that a task force of employees should be started to examine all the possible solutions suggested.

7. Which solution will solve the problem quickly and at least cost and inconvenience?
   - Again, at this point, because all the research has not been completed, you do not know the solution. But stress that the task force will search for the least expensive and least inconvenient solution.
   - This is an important paragraph in the letter. No one likes change. You have the obligation to your reader to indicate, if possible, that although the task force solution may mean change, it will be a positive change and shouldn't "hurt" that much.

By asking the seven key questions and putting bullet points under them, you've virtually written the letter!

Clumping

I once asked a CEO how he was quickly able to organize a report or a speech. He said, "I clump. I have three or four ideas. I put those ideas on paper. Then everything I think is relevant I clump under the idea I think it most applies to. Then I take my clumps, string them together and I have a report."

This clumping technique works well for people who just can't write an outline. By the way, there's nothing wrong with the inability to write an outline. Some people are frustrated and confused by the outline format.

An outline demands that you line all your ideas neatly up in a row, and many people, for many reasons, just don't think or write that "neatly."

The "clumping" approach offers a rough outline format that enables you to line up your information in the proper categories. It's a more free-wheeling approach, but if outlines don't work for you, chances are clumping will.

Note cards

A good way to use the clumping technique is to use note cards. Many writers use note cards to outline. They do so because, first, it forces them to stick to the main points. You can't write a whole lot on a three-by-five card. Like a postcard that can say no more than "Having a good time; wish you were here," writing on note cards forces you put down the main ideas and no more.

Note cards are great for outlining because, when all is said and done, outlining is about putting down the main ideas.

Here's the best way to use note cards. First, think of the key points you want to make. For example, you may want to sell a piece of software to a customer. You want the customer to know it's user-friendly, it can cut the cost of designing a product in half and it comes with a strong support network. Your first of three cards might look like this:

User-Friendly

The second card might read:

**Strong Software
Support**

And the third card might read:

Cost Savings

Now you can take these three cards and start three separate stacks. Under each card, you might have three or four others. Under the *Cost Savings* card, you might stack cards listing five key ways this software can save your customer money. Under *Strong Software Support*, you might stack cards listing four ways your product support is better than your competition's. See how it works?

By having three main points and backing each of them up with four or five key examples, you have your presentation all ready to go. Writing the report, memo or letter won't be that tough now because you have done the thinking ahead of time. Follow the note card "outline" you have designed, and your document will fall into place without hours of sweat.

Ernest Hemingway said, "Prose is architecture, not interior design." As this simple note card method demonstrates, if you get your thoughts lined up in a row, if you have the architectural drawings completed, the writing isn't that hard.

Focus

The most important part of any piece of writing is its focus. Your memo, letter or report may make many points—and all of them strong, excellent points, of course—but remember to concentrate on one main theme or idea. That idea may be as simple as why someone should buy your software.

When I was working for a newspaper, my editor often urged me to write the headline first. Doing so put the main idea into eight or 10 words and focused my writing on the task at hand. This method is also used in Hollywood concept-selling. When you pitch an idea to someone in Hollywood, that person wants the essence presented in one sentence: "This movie is a combination of *Rocky II* and *Driving Miss Daisy*."

Perhaps Norman Cousins said it best: "Effective communications, oral or written, depend absolutely on a clear understanding of one's purpose.

That purpose should be clearly identified. It should not be cluttered with extensive comment or side excursions. It should be developed point by point, with the rigorous attention to sequence and gradations of a professional bead-stringer at work."

How paragraphs can teach us focus

A paragraph is often a microcosm of an entire letter or report. Learning how a well-written paragraph is put together means beginning to understand how a well-written report is put together.

Like an entire report, the focus of the paragraph must be established. This can be done in the opening or closing line. But somewhere focus must be established. Study the selection below. Note how E.B. White builds example upon example so you walk away convinced of his point. The point, or focus, of this paragraph is strengthened by every point White makes.

"New York" by E.B. White

It is a miracle that New York works at all. The whole thing is implausible. Every time the residents brush their teeth, millions of gallons of water must be drawn from the Catskills and the hills of Westchester. When a young man in Manhattan writes a letter to his girl in Brooklyn, the love message gets blown to her through a pneumatic tube—pfft—just like that. The subterranean system of telephone cables, power lines, steam pipes, gas mains and sewer pipes is reason enough to abandon the island to the gods and the weevils. Every time an incision is made in the pavement, the noisy surgeons expose ganglia that are tangled beyond belief. By rights New York should have destroyed itself long ago, from panic or fire or rioting or failure of some vital supply line in its circulatory system or from some deep labyrinthine short circuit. Long ago the city should have experienced an insoluble traffic jam at some impossible bottleneck. It should have perished of hunger when food lines failed for a few days. It should have been wiped out by a plague starting in its slums or carried in by ships' rats. It should have been overwhelmed by the sea that licks at it from every side. The workers in its myriad cells should have succumbed to nerves from the fearful pall of smoke-fog that drifts over every few days from Jersey, blotting out all light at noon and leaving the high offices suspended, men groping and depressed, and the sense of world's end. It should have been touched in the head by the August heat and gone off its rocker.

You must establish the focus early. Don't be afraid to be too obvious. There is nothing wrong with coming right out and saying, "It is a miracle that New York works at all." A clear focus gives your readers a thorough understanding of what you are writing about.

An organizational checklist

When you are finished with your memo, letter or report, that's the best time to go back and ensure it's organized correctly. Here are 20 key things to check.

1. Can you follow the report from the opening paragraph to the closing paragraph as if it were a well-drawn map? Do you lead your readers into each section with clearly defined subheads? When you reach your destination, do your readers know that's where you were headed? For example, let's say you're writing instructions for your college-bound son on how to do laundry. Instead of two boring pages of text, you might divide it into three or four sections, such as "Sorting your laundry" and "Choosing hot or cold water." As you can see, your subheads help to organize your report and give your reader a good indication of what this section is about.

2. Did you tell the readers exactly what you were going to write about in your opening few lines or did you leave them guessing? Did you give a clear focus to the letter, report or memo?

3. Does your conclusion tell the reader what you said and emphasize the key points that must be reinforced? In short, a conclusion must consistently restate your main points, so they stick in your reader's mind.

4. Have you gotten all the details straight? I remember when I first started as a newspaper reporter, I misspelled one name in a story. The editor walked to my desk and dropped a big phone book on top of it. Clump! My whole desk shook. Then he said, "If you have *any* doubts about a name, look it up. And even if you *think* you know how to spell a name, double-check!" A misspelled name, a wrong dollar amount, a bad address, a misplaced decimal point—all of these can destroy the credibility of your report, letter or memo.

5. Do you have one idea per paragraph? We briefly touched upon this concept with the E.B. White example. Put your main idea at the beginning of the paragraph, then back it up.

6. Are your main ideas backed up with enough, but not too many, precise, easy-to-grasp examples? Remember the old Jewish saying: "When the horse is dead, get off." Don't use too many examples, and don't beat your reader over the head with them.

7. Does your memo, letter, proposal or report follow a straight line of thought, or have you taken detours into irrelevant topics?

8. Have you maintained a consistent argument, or have you "waffled," seeming unsure and incompetent?

9. Do your arguments justify the conclusion? Or in plain English, have you made your point?

10. Do you have too many topics under one subhead? Would it be better to "clump" these topics separately? Let's get back to our instructions on how to do laundry. Our first subhead is called "Sorting." Well, we assume that under this subhead we'll discuss sorting lights and darks, delicates and nondelicates, and so forth. But after we have discussed this, if we start talking about going down to the store and choosing a laundry detergent, it's obviously time we move on to a new subhead.

11. Have you presented your views in a professional manner without trashing others' views; have you been fair and objective?

12. Have you generalized too much, e.g., saying, "Sales will reach a new high in September," without giving specific numbers and important details to back up your point?

13. Do you have your facts right? Are your sources reliable, or are you quoting your mother-in-law again who believes anything she sees on *Wheel of Fortune*?

14. Did you use all the high-tech tools, like spell checker?

15. Did you have someone else read the document and give you a good outsider's opinion?

16. Does the document tell your readers why actions will benefit them, not you?

17. Does your document appear professional, with lots of white space, professional titles and clear, concise sentence structure?

18. Would you be proud to show it to Mrs. Grammercy, your fifth-grade teacher?

19. Did you go back and look at the key elements of the report? Did you go step-by-step through the report, making sure that all the key things your readers need are in that report?

20. Finally: Is it in English? Have you used short powerful words that get your point across, or have you slipped into vague business terms that you hope will cover your lack of knowledge?

Chapter 1 summary

It's obvious that I am a strong believer in organizing a report, letter or memo before you begin to write it. If you don't organize, you are in danger of leaving out important points. Plus you run the risk of boring your readers with what I call "warm up" paragraphs. With a well-organized outline before you, you should be focused in the very first sentence. Finally, here's a good way to tell if you are organized and getting to the point: Cross out the first couple of paragraphs of what you have just written. Does the letter lose anything? If not, you need to go back and reorganize.

2

Clichés, jargon, etc: a few words on words

"It's the itsy-bitsy, teensy-weensy things that beat you."
—Bear Byrant

In the last section, we discussed how to get organized. Now, in the next two sections, we're going to discuss a variety of sins that can make you look like an amateur writer.

Perhaps the best way to describe the next two sections is to say that "little things mean a lot." We will describe a host of writing sins ranging from clichés to weak verbs, from excessive use of adjectives to excessive use of adverbs.

Each piece of advice is important because writing sins do add up. A cliché slipped in here, a constant use of weak verbs or a simple lack of sentence variety all add up to one message: You didn't think what you were writing was worth the time and effort needed to avoid such things.

A good piece of writing is like a well-running, dependable engine. When you step on the gas, the engine responds quickly and gives you enough power to get you to your destination. When you want to idle for a while, the engine idles perfectly, without hesitation or unnecessarily rich exhaust blowing out of the tailpipe.

But let's say things start to go wrong with the engine. The fuel-air mixture is just a bit too rich, the timing is only a second off, and the fuel filter is slightly clogged. These are only small items, that's true. But add them together and you have a very rough-running engine you won't trust to get you across town.

This same analogy extends to writing. Just one adverb or adjective too many, a misplaced comma, a misspelled word, a cliché tossed in... again, all these are small sins. But add them up and your writing will no longer purr like a finely tuned engine. It will sputter and wheeze. Your reader may not trust your writing or what you are trying to say.

Although I must apologize for the extended analogy, the point is valid. Pay special attention to the next two sections.

By learning to recognize clichés and jargon, you can avoid them. And that will give your writing a freshness your readers will appreciate.

Clichés (or you've buttered your bread, now lie in it)

What's wrong with clichés? Simply this: They are worn-out phrases that require no thought. They say to your readers, "At this point in my writing my brain went into cruise control. I really didn't give this section much thought; I just slipped into a tired, overused way of writing."

For example, besides stringing a bunch of clichés together, what does this memo really tell you?

Your new agenda: Be proactive and interface with customers. Start networking. Finalize sales. Rack up the done deals that will impact the bottom line. Vis-à-vis our competitors, we've got world-class, state-of-the-art, user-friendly products. That's our competitive edge. We've also got the know-how for a major breakthrough to put us on the fast track to a win-win situation. We need your hands-on input, so start the sales dialogue now. Putting it off is a no-brainer.

How about this opening to a brochure? It doesn't tell you anything about the business, but it does trot out every cliché.

On the eve of a new age in business, America's industries have been doing a great deal of soul-searching. They are looking for innovative partnerships and fresh perspectives on building lasting relationships with customers.

When the dust settles, chances are that Acme Inc. will be found at the center of a new, market-driven industry grounded in customer relationships. Combining a fresh-thinking vision with state-of-the-art technology, Acme Inc. delivers a cutting-edge advantage to those businesses striving to lead the pack into the next century.

Busy readers are now two paragraphs into the brochure and have been given no facts, figures—in short no real information—about the company. How much longer will they put up with this? If they're halfway intelligent, they've already chucked the brochure.

As a former speechwriter, I am amazed at the number of clichés people slip into their speeches. These include:

- We're here to chart a new course for this company.
- This is the most challenging time in history, both for our industry and our company.
- The competition has never been fiercer.
- These new products will turn this industry on its ear.
- The name of the game is teamwork.
- We must not only work harder, we must work smarter.
- I can assure you that the management team is behind you every step of the way.
- It's a whole new world out there.
- We won't be satisfied until we're the Number 1 company in the industry.
- The future of this company lies with you.
- We gather tonight in a world of changes...
- And so tonight, let us resolve...
- We must do more.
- It's time to stop. (I bet you wish I would by now.)
- We must set tough, world-class standards. (The phrase "world-class" is no longer world-class and should be retired.)
- It's time to stop ignoring...
- I know it will be difficult.
- To those who would...
- It will not be easy.
- But there is a long, hard road ahead.
- We'll all have to put our heads together.
- And let's be honest.
- My fellow Americans...
- Therefore, I urge you...
- So, I ask you to remember...
- And so I say to you tonight...

Quite simply, clichés show you're not taking care with or showing interest in the writing. And, just think, if the above clichés were banned from every speech or document, something truly exciting might happen. The audience (listening or reading) might stay awake, and the presenter might get to the point a lot more quickly. To further heighten your awareness of clichés, a more extensive list follows. Please avoid them. Your readers will thank you!

A list of clichés

The right to a fair shake	Pick up the tab
The lion's share	Swept under the rug
We have no earthly idea	Looking over his shoulder
Before we rush headlong	It remains to be seen
We want to draw the line	The cold facts are
Let's keep all avenues open	In for rough sledding
We can close the gap	It can't be established overnight
That's a pretty big "if"	A sense of direction
By the same token	You get the picture
A far-reaching effect	When the dust settles
Moved to greener pastures	The powers that be
It's a step forward	It seems to boil down to
There's a 50/50 chance	Gets a lot of mileage out of
Grappling with the question	It has fallen on deaf ears
Caused quite an uproar	Just in the nick of time
Don't want to rock the boat	The handwriting on the wall
Get the ball rolling	Out of our hair

A caveat!

By the way, there is nothing wrong with using one of these expressions now and then. Just so you don't beat it to death. (Whoops, a cliché! See how those stinkers slip in everywhere?) The real danger is not in using a cliché every now and then; it is in building your entire correspondence on them. I have seen letters that are merely one long cliché starting with "We must throw light on the subject" and ending with "The bottom line is..."

If your writing reflects nothing but clichés, what does that tell me about your thinking?

Note: What follows is a piece called *The Cliché Expert Takes the Stand.* It is a valuable exercise to read out loud. Doing so gives you a sense of the inane way clichés sound and the way they merely echo in someone's brain without leaving a permanent impression. Also note that the piece was written in 1935, proving that writers come and go, but clichés hang around forever.

"The Cliché Expert Takes the Stand" by Frank Sullivan

Q. Mr. Arbuthnot, you are an expert in the use of the cliché, are you not?

A. Yes, sir, I am a certified public cliché expert.

Q. In that case would you be good enough to answer a few questions on the use and application of the cliché in ordinary speech and writing?

A. I should only be glad to do so.

Q. Thank you. Now, just for the record—you live in New York?

A. I like to visit New York but I wouldn't live here if you gave me the place.

Q. Then where do you live?

A. Any old place I hang my hat is home sweet home to me.

Q. What is your age?

A. I am fat, fair and forty.

Q. And your occupation?

A. Well, after burning the midnight oil at an institution of higher learning, I was for a time a tiller of the soil. Then I went down to the sea in ships for a while, and later, at various times, I have been a guardian of the law, a gentleman of the Fourth Estate, a poet at heart, a bon vivant and raconteur, a prominent clubman and man about town, an eminent—

Q. Just what is your occupation at the moment, Mr. Arbuthnot?

A. At the moment I am an unidentified man of about forty, shabbily clad.

Q. Now then, Mr. Arbuthnot, what kind of existence do you, as a cliché expert, lead?

A. A precarious existence.

Q. And what do you do to lead a precarious existence?

A. I eke it out.

Q. How do you cliché experts reveal yourselves, Mr. Arbuthnot?

A. In our true colors, of course.

Q. Now, Mr. Arbuthnot, when you are naked, you are...

A. Stark naked.

Q. In what kind of daylight?

A. Broad daylight.

Q. What kind of outsider are you?

A. I'm a rank outsider.

Q. You are as sober as a...

A. A judge.

Q. And when you are drunk...

A. I have lots of leeway there. I can be drunk as a coot, or a lord, or an owl, or a fool—

Q. Very good, Mr. Arbuthnot. Now how brown are you?

A. As brown as a berry?

Q. Ever seen a brown berry?

A. Oh, no. Were I to see a brown berry, I should be frightened.

Q. To what extent?

A. Out of my wits.

Q. How about the fate of Europe?

A. It's hanging in the balance, of course.

Q. What goes with "pure"?

A. Simple.

Q. Thank you, Mr. Arbuthnot. What kind of beauties do you like?

A. Raving beauties.

Q. How generous are you?

A. I'm generous to a fault.

Q. How is corruption these days?

A. Oh, rife, as usual.

Q. How do you point?

A. I point with pride, I view with alarm, and I yield to no man...

Q. And when you are taken, you are taken...

A. Aback.

Q. I see. I think that everyone who has listened to you today will be a better cliché-user for having heard you. Thank you, very, very, much.

A. Thank *you*, Mr. Steurer. It's been a pleasure, I assure you, and I was only too glad to oblige.

Frank Sullivan, "The Cliché Expert Takes the Stand," abridged from *The New Yorker*, Aug. 31, 1935.

———

Okay, you *can* use clichés cleverly

Wait, is this guy nuts? He tells us to avoid clichés like the plague (hey, nice cliché there, buddy), and then he says we can use them sometimes? Put this guy away! No, I'm not nuts. The sign of an amateur is that he or she will use a cliché as if it were exciting. Clichés can't be fresh, but they can be used in fresh ways. For example, a bad writer will use a line such as, "As Calvin Coolidge said, 'The business of America is business.' That's as true today as it was sixty-five years ago."

A good writer would say, "Calvin Coolidge once said, 'The business of America is business.' That was a long time ago. Today, the business of America is corporate raiding, white knights, golden parachutes, greenmail, and junk bonds." This example works because the writer cleverly updated a comatose cliché.

Many times a twisted cliché can get a laugh. For example, you might write, "You made your bed; now lie in it." Ho hum. But twist that cliché to "You've buttered your bread; now lie in it," and you have left your readers smiling.

Jargon: the kissing cousin of the cliché

Luckily, if you want to avoid thinking about your writing, you now have a new way of doing it. You can use jargon instead of clichés. Just as you can with clichés, you can plug in jargon and have an instant letter or report. The fact that no one understands it doesn't matter. It looks impressive.

And jargon is easy to write. In fact, take the list below, select a word from each of the three columns and you have an instant phrase! For instance, you might like "total organizational flexibility." Let's look at this time-saving—but ineffective—way of writing:

1. integrated	1. management	1. options
2. total	2. organizational	2. flexibility
3. systematized	3. monitored	3. capability
4. parallel	4. reciprocal	4. mobility
5. functional	5. digital	5. programming
6. responsive	6. logic	6. concept
7. optical	7. transitional	7. time-phase
8. synchronized	8. incremental	8. projection
9. compatible	9. third-generation	9. hardware
10. balanced	10. policy	10. contingency

What are you trying to say?
Call a spade "a spade"

Why should you call a spade "a spade"? Consider the many people who just can't call a thing by its correct name. The U.S. State Department doesn't kill people, for instance; it causes "arbitrary deprivation of life."

The U.S. Air Force calls a Titan II missile, tipped with a nine-megaton nuclear bomb, "a very large, potentially disruptive re-entry system." Well, I admit, it would disrupt my life.

In one hospital, patients don't die. Instead, they suffer "negative patient care outcome."

One grocery store doesn't have spoiled fruit or vegetables. They have "distressed produce." California has eliminated ambulances. Instead they have "major incident response units." But the winners have to be the economists who believe we no longer have recessions. Instead we have "a period of advanced negative economic growth."

People don't get fired anymore. Instead they get:

outplaced	dehired
downsized	degrown
rightsized	deselected
indefinitely idled	decruited
redundancy-eliminated	excessed
involuntarily separated	transitioned
skill-mix adjusted	vocationally relocated
work force imbalance-corrected	selectively separated
chemistry-changed	transition-coerced
departure-negotiated	executive-culled
redeployed	personnel surplus reduced
destaffed	career assessed and reemployed
	fumigated

Let's communicate

The following article of mine, which appeared in *The Wall Street Journal*, highlights the communication barriers jargon establishes.

Eschew That Paradigm! Drop the Jargon

The first rule of communication is that different groups and different people can speak the same language and thereby understand one another. This lesson should be easy enough to grasp, particularly for consultants who are paid highly to improve communications in a company. But when some world-renowned consultants came to our utilities company several months back, few of us were prepared for the communication breakdown that was about to hit.

The problem started small: a word sprinkled here or there in the managers' conversation. Someone felt "empowered"; someone else was breaking free of "paradigms."

Then it spread. Managers started speaking in tongues. You'd round a corner and you'd hear a manager say: "Through virtual leadership, I took the cultural determinants and broke through."

Not that my company was innocent to begin with. Most aren't. Managers typically avoid strong verbs and "utilize" words. And corporations thrive on acronyms. I once met an employee who proudly announced to me that she had STD. I beat a retreat, unsure of what sexually transmitted disease she had. Later, I discovered she meant short-term disability.

Luckily, we always had our line workers to keep our corporate lingo simple and direct. Whenever they dropped a tool, they yelled "headache" to warn people below. To "hang a pot" meant to install a new meter. To "hook up a buggy" meant to hook up a portable generator. And to "torch your shorts" was a clever phrase for receiving a mild electric shock.

Then the consultants came in droves, dragging their charts and graphs and their vocabularies! Our company became completely jargonized. The words slithered everywhere.

The magic word seemed to be "strategic." A feeling grew among managers that if you attached the word "strategic" to anything, it would get approved. I even saw a memo discussing "strategic dreaming."

Oh, there were a few brave managers who strategically resisted by wearing earplugs and nodding happily at everything the consultants said. Unfortunately, nodding happily translated into approval for a new consulting project. So they stopped wearing earplugs and the jargon seized them too.

It was insidious. You couldn't sit in the cafeteria without hearing about "excellerated" cultural change, cultural "intervention," three-stream models, architectural rigor and discipline, people value, integrated strategic change and core efficiencies. Managers would chat happily for hours, a glazed, contented look on their faces, while they chowed down their "cultural vitamins."

But one day, barricaded in my office, wearing a copy of Strunk and White's Elements of Style *around my neck like a protective charm, I had a thought. Surely, the consultant psychobabble hadn't seduced our line workers. Surely common sense survived among the line crews and customer service representatives.*

I ventured forth. There was hope! The line employees gave me these quotes:

"It's really frustrating. This consultant language has developed into a language of its own. It really alienates us. I have to get out my dictionary just to understand my manager."

"I feel we should pay someone to translate for us."

"My manager is indoctrinated in this language. He doesn't speak English anymore. He doesn't even have to think what it means. He just types it in and there it is."

"It's like they're some elite group that speaks French, when the rest of us speak American."

"If someone walked into this company, they'd be thinking we speak Martian."

"You start thinking you should know what these terms mean, so you don't say anything."

Perhaps the light at the end of the tunnel wasn't a consultant brandishing a flashlight. The front line was still holding out, waiting for common sense or at least clear English to return to the management ranks.

They were also delivering a message that none of us should ever forget: If you want to change your company's culture, speak the employees' language, not the consultants'.

I returned to corporate headquarters refreshed. But images of "energizing visions" and "visions congruencies" still darted through my head.

I thought I could hold out. Then "empowerments" and "visions" started creeping into my own conversation. I had to get someone to listen to the line employees! I searched the hallways for a sympathetic manager.

But the empty hallways only echoed my running feet. I stumbled into a large meeting room. The managers were kneeling on the floor, bowing before a large icon of the letters spelling out the name of a famous consulting firm.

I yelled, but they couldn't hear me. Their chant of "Strategic, Strategic, Strategic" drowned out my screams.

How can I be free of jargon?

Is there a 12-step program I can attend?

So how do you know when you're using jargon? If people get a glazed look on their faces, as if you've shown them one too many baby pictures or vacation slides, that might be your first clue. Also, if you get no response, if they just sit there and nod and nod and finally nod off, there's another clue.

To help you overcome the *jargon affliction*, here is a list of just some of the jargon floating around today. But beware. Jargon is like a virus. Just when you think you have a strong immune system, a new virus comes along. Or in the case of language, a new bit of jargon comes along.

But study this list. It will help cleanse you of jargon, and soon you may be seen in public, leading a decent life again.

Words and phrases to use with caution

A quantum leap
A sense of urgency
Accountability
Alternative architectures
An edge over (the competition)
Anchor (use as a verb)
Architectural rigor and
    discipline
Arena
Backward integration
Benchmark
Benefit streams
Best practice
Blueprinting
Both internal and external
Boundaryless behavior
Break-out
Breakthrough
Business case analysis
Cascading feedback
Case for action
Clean-slate philosophy
Coaching up

Code of conduct
Collaborative conceptualization
Collocated
Command and control
Commitment reduction process
Continuous improvement
Core process redesign
Core team
Cost savings/cost management
Critical business process
Critical dependencies
Cross functional
Cross-sectional
Cultural determinates
Cultural diversity
Cultural intervention
Cultural warriors
Cutover
De-fragmentation
De-selection process
Departmental boundaries
Departmentalized
Do more with less

Dramatic!
Early start initiatives
Employee concerns
Empowerment
Enabler
Energizing
Energizing visions
Environment
Error-free product
Essential enabler
Excellerated
Excited and inspired people
Externalizes
Flavor-of-the-month
Focus
Focus group
Forced ranking
Fostering an environment
Fragmented
From the outside-in
Front-line
Functional rationalization
Functionality bundles
Fundamental analysis
Generalists
Get on board
Hand-offs
High performing culture
Horizontal priority
Incrementalism
Interactive communication
Jump start (verb or noun)
Leadership principles
Legendary service
Life design
Living the vision
Maintenance drivers
Measurement tool
Mind map
Mission critical
Model (noun or verb)

More calculated risk-taking
More risk-taking
Move the needle
Multi-faceted individuals
Multi-functional
Multi-tasking organization
Need for speed
Off the scale
Out the door
Ownership
Participative
Partnering
Passionately
Performance enhancement
Personal accountability
Personal development
Pockets within the
    organization
Point blank
Pollution prevention
Positive confrontation
Premier corporate citizen
Proactive
Process
Process constituencies
Process improvement
Process map
Process modeling
Process team
Progressive chaos
Quick hit
Rapid pace of change
Re-design
Re-engineer
Re-invent
Re-structure
Re-think
Reactive
Remediation
Reorchestration
Reskilling

Revolutionary change
Rewards and recognition
Road map
Seamless
Seemingly unreachable
   targets
Self-empowerment
Self-directed
Six sigma (a six-sigma
   performer)
Skill set
Smarter
Steering committee
Step into another arena
Strategic plan objectives
Streamlining
Suboptimization
Team (noun, verb or adjective)
Technology-enabled visioning

The need to decrease our
   cultural viscosity
Their own agendas
360-degree feedback
Three-stream model
Tough but achievable (goals)
Transitioning
Trust and mutual respect
200-percent accountability
Undaunted
Unnecessary distribution
Value-added
Vertical discipline systems
Vertical slice
Virtual leadership
Vision congruencies
Winning team
Work drivers
Z-teams

"Writing is easy. All you have to do is cross out the wrong words."

—Mark Twain

Clutter...clutter...clutter...

Consider these statistics: In the United States we have 260,000 billboards, 11,520 newspapers, 11,556 periodicals, 27,000 video stores, more than 500 million radios and more than 100 million computers. Ninety-eight percent of American homes have a television set; more than 40,000 new book titles are published a year; and every day in America, 41 million photographs are taken. If that is not enough, more than 60 billion pieces of junk mail stuff our collective mailboxes.

The average American is exposed to about 3,000 commercial messages, from newspapers to billboards, per day. *And every year more than 83,329 pieces of paper cross the average executive's desk!*

Note I have not even mentioned e-mail or cable television. The point is that through lightwaves, airwaves, computer banks, telephone wires, television cables, satellites and printing presses, we are drowning in information.

And with all this information, getting your message across is tough.

It's even tougher if you jam your message up with clutter. Look at this passage. Who has time to figure it out? Who wants to?

> *The fact that he had not made up his mind about the personnel problem prior to his departure showed he was not in the best of health. In the final analysis and in the foreseeable or near future, he must address the problem on the part of each and every one of us. If he does not remember that a large percentage of personnel will put in no appearance in the month of August....*

Whoa! What is that paragraph all about? Let's try writing it in English.

> *He seems to have been sick because he did not decide to keep or fire Louise before he left. He knows we need an answer before August, when many of us take vacations....*

Isn't the second paragraph a lot easier to read? The problem with the first paragraph is simply this: The writer is being blindsided by the "clutter factor." Whenever one word will do, he puts in three or four. If only he could use short, simple words to get his point across. If he did that, his readers might even scan the paragraph to get the meaning without drowning in a sea of verbiage.

The problem with clutter is that it sneaks in. Half the time we don't even realize we are using clutter words. Instead of writing, "We expect to open three new offices," we write, "In terms of the future, we expect to have three new office openings." Instead of saying, "She teaches fourth grade," we write, "She teaches on the fourth-grade level." And instead of saying "civil rights," we say, "in the area of civil rights."

One day a manager tossed a report on my desk. He said, "I keep getting reports like this from my staff. I have to reread the damn things over and over just to see what they're trying to say. I must waste eight hours every week just trying to figure out these reports. Plus, they're way too long. Why can't they say the same thing in one page, instead of three?"

Here is one paragraph of the report he showed me.

> *The results of interviews and other discussions with I&C personnel indicate that most of the personnel errors related to the conduct of Surveillance Testing are being made by a relatively limited number of people. The consensus was that when field personnel make "too many" mistakes or become "known for their errors," management has a tendency to place these poorer performers in less directly consequential jobs....*

I did pity the manager. But if the writer of this lengthy report had watched her "clutter factor," she could have rewritten the first paragraph this way:

Interviews with I&C personnel show that only a few people are making most of the Surveillance Testing errors. Management tends to place these people in jobs that don't have important consequences.

A sample clutter letter

Here is a sample clutter letter. Cross out the clutter phrases.

Dear Bill:

As you can see and may have already heard, I have joined The Excell Group Inc. as the Director of Government Relations for both state and federal policy. There is life after years of public service, and I am looking forward to putting my experience and network of contacts to work on behalf of our clients.

I certainly don't need to tell you how federal and state legislation or regulation can increase the cost of operating your business. With my knowledge of local, state and federal experience in government, our company can be of benefit to your company in the area of anticipating and shaping legislation that you may be concerned about.

Although you may already have someone in Washington D.C. and at the Arizona State legislature for your company, I would like to discuss the possibility of augmenting your existing plan. I may bring to your team or strategy a different perspective or different circle of influence to advance your issues. Working one's way through the bureaucracy and government regulations can be a daunting task, even for the most experienced staff. Knowing who to approach on issues is often the answer to solving a difficult problem.

My office will call you to find some time I might sit down with you to discuss the possibility of The Excell Group's supporting your legislative needs. If you have some immediate issues please don't hesitate to call me at 555-2929. I look forward to the opportunity to talk to you.

Sincerely,

Now here is the same letter with the clutter phrases in bold. Did you catch all of them?

> *Dear Bill:*
> *__As you can see and may have already heard,__ I have joined The Excell Group Inc. as the Director of Government Relations for both state and federal policy. There is life after years of public service, and I am looking forward to putting my experience and network of contacts to work on behalf of our clients.*
> *__I certainly don't need to tell you how__ federal and state legislation __or regulation__ can increase the cost of operating your business. With my knowledge of local, state and federal __experience in__ government, __our company can be of benefit to your company in the area of anticipating and shaping__ legislation that __you may be concerned about__.*
> *Although you may __already__ have someone in Washington D.C. and at the Arizona State legislature for your company, __I would like to discuss the possibility of augmenting your existing plan. I may bring to your team or strategy__ a different perspective or different circle of influence to advance your issues. Working one's way through the bureaucracy __and government regulations__ can be __a__ daunting __task__, even for the most experienced staff. Knowing who to approach on issues is often the answer to solving a difficult problem.*
> *My office will call you to find some time __I might sit down with you__ to __discuss the possibility__ of The Excell Group's supporting your legislative needs. If you have some immediate issues, please __don't hesitate to__ call me at 555-2929. I __look forward to the opportunity__ to talk to you.*
> *Sincerely,*

Below, the letter is rewritten. Note the way a well-chosen verb can often eliminate many clutter words.

> *Dear Bill:*
> *I have joined The Excell Group Inc. as the Director of Government Relations for both state and federal policy. There is life after years of public service, and perhaps my experience and network of contacts may benefit your company.*
> *Federal and state legislation can increase the cost of operating your business. My knowledge of local, state and federal government can help your company anticipate and shape legislation that may concern you.*

Although you may have someone in Washington D.C. and in Phoenix lobbying for your company, I will bring a different perspective and a different sphere of influence to advance your issues. Working one's way through the bureaucracy can be daunting, even for the most experienced staff. Knowing who to approach on issues is often the answer to solving a difficult problem.

My office will call to discuss The Excell Group's supporting your legislative needs. If you have some immediate issues, please call me at 555-2929.

Sincerely,

Note that this letter is much shorter and gets to the point much more quickly. If you were a busy executive, which one would you prefer to read?

A list of words to avoid

Below is a list of common "clutter phrases" that can sneak into your writing. Beware. They're everywhere!

Clutter	Better
the fact that	that
made up his mind	decided
prior to, in advance of	before
best of health	finally
the foreseeable future	soon
on the part of	by
with the exception of	except
the absence of	no
the question as to whether	whether
draw your attention to	show you
in the event of	if
in order to	to
filled to capacity	full
in spite of the fact	although
the month of May	in May
put in an appearance	appear
at this time	now
in short supply	scarce
in the majority of instances	usually
a percentage of	some
did not remember	forgot
ahead of schedule	early
accordingly	so

Your turn to rewrite clutter words

(Answers are provided on page 52.)

Clutter	Better
great majority	_____
for this reason	_____
in close proximity	_____
personally reviewed	_____
serious crisis	_____
subject matter	_____
contingent upon	_____
utilized	_____
a number of	_____
at the rate of	_____
bring to a conclusion	_____
connected together	_____
due to the fact that	_____
end result	_____
in the direction of	_____
in the foreseeable future	_____
advanced warning	_____
not in a position to	_____
repeat again	_____
a small number of	_____
enclosed herewith	_____
in the event that	_____
without further delay	_____
time of day	_____
mutual cooperation	_____
merged together	_____
brief in duration	_____
basic fundamentals	_____
at a later date	_____
ask the question	_____
general public	_____
plan in advance	_____

Eliminate clutter words

Sometimes there is simply no need to *replace* a clutter word or phrase—you can just cross it out. Here is a list of clutter phrases you can cross out whenever they appear in a sentence.

- I would hope
- I would like to express my appreciation
- As I am sure you know
- As you are aware
- As you know
- It is my intention

- In such a manner as to
- As I was recently noting
- We wish to state
- It has come to my attention
- Regarding the matter of
- Pursuant to your request

"The difference between the almost right word and the right word is really a large matter—'tis the difference between the lightning bug and the lightning."

—Mark Twain

Use simple words!

Many of us are leading double lives. When we chat with someone, we act normal. We say, "He quit his job." Or we say, "I'm going to buy that." But when we sit down in front of a piece of paper, our alter ego takes over. We lead a second life. We "purchase" things; we "resign" positions; we don't "use" but "utilize" things. We don't have a method. No! We have a "methodology." Something has happened to us. That blank piece of paper has taken over our brains, and we can't use simple, direct language.

For example, look at this flyer sent to various businesses to help them deal with pests:

> *To help eliminate the problem of pests, one long-lasting product that never loses its potency is common Boric Acid. Utilizing the powder form in strategic areas has been proven quite effective in alleviating a future problem.*

I think the writer was simply trying to say, "Sprinkle Boric Acid in key areas. It will kill pests."

Then there's the scientist who wrote, "The biota exhibited a 100 percent mortality rate." He was trying to say, "All the fish died."

And I love this one. During the early days of World War II, when city officials were worried about air raids, "black-outs" were required. So a city worker put signs everywhere that read, "Illumination is required to be extinguished on these premises after nightfall." Of course, he meant, "Lights out after dark."

Write to express, not to impress

When writing, remember this important rule: *Write to express, not to impress!* If you write to impress and not express, trouble can result, as this story shows:

> *A plumber once wrote to the Bureau of Standards, saying he found hydrochloric acid excellent for cleaning drains. He asked the Bureau if it was safe. The answer: "The efficiency of hydrochloric acid is indisputable, but the chlorine residue is incompatible with metallic permanence."*
>
> *The plumber wrote back thanking the Bureau and expressing his pleasure that they agreed with him.*
>
> *The Bureau people were so alarmed at being misunderstood that they replied with a second letter: "We cannot assume responsibility for the production of toxic and noxious residues with hydrochloric acid, and we suggest you use an alternative procedure."*
>
> *The plumber wrote again, saying that he was glad they were keeping in touch, he was happy to know about their responsibilities, and he was continuing to use HCL.*
>
> *The Bureau finally sent out a fax:*
>
> *"DON'T USE HCL! IT EATS THE HELL OUT OF THE PIPES."*

One short word can save your copy

John Caples, a famous advertising man who was considered the best copywriter in the field, said this about simple, direct language: "Sometimes you can change a word and increase the pulling power of an ad. Once, I changed the word *repair* to *fix* and the ad pulled 20 percent more."

In other words, keep your writing short and concise. As Professor William Strunk said in *The Elements of Style:*

> *"Vigorous writing is concise. A sentence should contain no unnecessary words, a paragraph no unnecessary sentences, for the same reason that a drawing should have no unnecessary lines and a machine no unnecessary parts. This does not mean that the writer make all his sentences short, or that he avoid all detail and treat his subjects only in outline, but that every word tell."*

Here's another way to see how effective short, powerful words are. What do you notice about the quotes below?

- "Don't fire until you see the whites of their eyes."
- "These are times that try men's souls."
- "I regret that I have only one life to give to my country."
- "The only thing we have to fear is fear itself."

That's right, these quotes live in history because they're simple and direct. Yet if short words and short quotes are so powerful, why do we often resort to the biggest, baddest word we can find? Simply, we're afraid others will not think we're intelligent if we write in clear, simple English. Trust me. That's not true.

Simplicity equals grace

Below is a speech by Chief Joseph, chief of the Nez Percé American Indian tribe who surrendered to the U.S. Army in October of 1877. It is one of the most powerful speeches ever uttered. But note, once again, that its beauty does not come from long words strung together. Rather its beauty comes from simplicity and sincerity.

I am tired of fighting. Our chiefs are killed. Looking Glass is dead. Toohulsote is dead. The old men are all dead. It is the young men who say no and yes. He who led the young men is dead. It is cold and we have no blankets. The little children are freezing to death. My people, some of them, have run away to the hills and have no blankets, no food; no one knows where they are—perhaps freezing to death. I want to have time to look for my children and see how many I can find. Maybe I shall find them among the dead. Hear me, my chiefs, I am tired; my heart is sick and sad. From where the sun stands, I will fight no more forever.

Remember, keep it short

Oliver Wendell Holmes once explained why he wrote his legal opinions standing up. He said, "If I sit down, I write a long opinion and don't come to the point as quickly as I could. If I stand up, I write as long as my knees hold out. When my knees give out, I know it's time to stop."

Remember to keep it short. Look at the great documents that contain very few words:

The Lord's Prayer: 56 words

Lincoln's Gettysburg Address: 268 words

The Declaration of Independence: 1,322 words

Compare them to:

A Government regulation on the sale of cabbage: 26,911 words

Latin words vs. Anglo-Saxon

Some words have an Anglo-Saxon base. Others have a Latin base. As a rule of thumb, use the Anglo-Saxon words. They tend to be more direct. The list below illustrates the difference:

Anglo-Saxon	Latin
woman	female
happiness	felicity
bill	beak
friendship	amity
help	aid
folk	people
hearty	cordial
holy	saintly
deep	profound
lonely	solitary
begin	commence
hide	conceal
feed	nourish
hinder	prevent
leave	abandon
die	perish
house	domicile
moon	lunar
watery	aquatic
timely	temporal
daily	diurnal
truthful	veracious
kingly	regal
youthful	juvenile
weighty	ponderous
share	portion
wretched	miserable
same	identical
killing	homicide
manly	virile
tale	story
up	ascend
put out	extinguish

Select the simple word over the Latin word

As you can see, the Latin word is longer and makes understanding you more difficult for your reader. The following list can help you find a good, direct word to replace a "stylish" word. Notice that the pompous words are all three or more syllables. The word you replace it with should be no longer than two syllables. (Answers are provided on page 53.)

1. abandon _____
2. fundamental _____
3. abolish _____
4. illustrate _____
5. accomplish _____
6. indicate _____
7. accumulate _____
8. institute _____
9. adequate _____
10. liquidate _____
11. beneficial _____
12. maximize _____
13. characteristic _____
14. neutralize _____
15. commitment _____
16. objective _____
17. compensation _____
18. obligate _____
19. component _____
20. participate _____
21. demonstrate _____
22. proportion _____
23. discontinue _____
24. regulation _____
25. encounter _____
26. remittance _____
27. endeavor _____
28. repudiate _____
29. enumerate _____
30. severance _____
31. expedite _____
32. subsequent _____
33. fabricate _____
34. terminate _____
35. fluctuate _____
36. verify _____

Remember, Bloom's law of explosives, "If some is good, more is better," does not apply to clutter words.

Also remember the words of Donald Hall, the writer: "Less is more, in prose as in architecture."

Glossary of Administration

Of course, to be fair, there are times when we don't want to communicate directly. We want to put people off, avoid them for a while, hide the fact we messed up. Thankfully, the Michigan School Board has come up with a *Glossary of Administration* to help us miscommunicate:

It's in the process.	We forgot about it until now.
We'll look into this.	Meanwhile, you may forget it too.
Program	A project requiring more than one phone call.
Project	A word that makes a minor job seem major.
Under consideration	Never heard about it until now.
Under active consideration	We're trying to locate the correspondence.
We're making a survey.	We need more time to think up an answer.
Let's get together on this.	You're probably as mixed up as I am.
Reliable source	The man you just met.
Informed source	The guy who told the man you just met.
Unimpeachable source	The fellow who started the rumor.
Activate	Make more copies and add names to the memo.
Implement	Hire more people and expand the office.
Consultant	Anyone with a briefcase more than 50 miles from home.
Take this up at our next meeting.	That will give you time to forget.
Note and initial	Let's spread the responsibility.
Forwarded for consideration	You hold the bag for a while.
We can go over this at lunch.	It's time we ate on your expense account.

Chapter 2 summary

We've gone through two important sections now. The first taught us how to get organized. The second one discussed basic steps we can all take to keep our writing concise and understandable.

The next section has to do with style. Baseball great Ted Williams once said, "Don't ever let anyone monkey with your swing." But Ted was able to say that only after years of practicing and perfecting his swing.

This is the section in which we "monkey with your swing." We aim to move your writing style up a few notches and help you reach a higher level of expertise. Simple "subject-verb, subject-verb" writing, with no sense of rhythm, was okay for the minors. But now you're moving into the majors, and just as a good pitcher needs to mix up his stuff to stay up in "the Show," you need a wide repertoire of writing skills at your disposal.

In short, you need more than one arrow in your quiver of writing skills, and here's where we start to expand those skills, to add those arrows.

Answers to *Your turn to rewrite clutter words,* page 44

Clutter	**Better**
great majority	majority
for this reason	because
in close proximity	near
personally reviewed	reviewed
serious crisis	crisis
subject matter	subject
contingent upon	upon
utilized	used
a number of	many
at the rate of	per
bring to a conclusion	conclude
connected together	connected
due to the fact that	because
end result	result
in the direction of	toward
in the foreseeable future	in the future
advanced warning	warning
not in a position to	can't
repeat again	repeat
a small number of	few
enclosed herewith	enclosed
in the event that	if (or when)
without further delay	now
time of day	time
mutual cooperation	cooperation
merged together	merged
brief in duration	brief
basic fundamentals	fundamentals
at a later date	later
ask the question	ask
general public	public
plan in advance	plan

Answers to *Select the simple word over the Latin word,* page 49

1. abandon: leave
2. fundamental: basic
3. abolish: end
4. illustrate: show
5. accomplish: complete
6. indicate: show
7. accumulate: add up
8. institute: start
9. adequate: fair
10. liquidate: clear
11. beneficial: good
12. maximize: increase
13. characteristic: typical
14. neutralize: stop
15. commitment: pledge
16. objective: goal
17. compensation: pay
18. obligate: must

19. component: part
20. participate: join
21. demonstrate: show
22. proportion: part
23. discontinue: stop
24. regulation: rule
25. encounter: meet
26. remittance: payment
27. endeavor: try
28. repudiate: deny
29. enumerate: list
30. severance: quit
31. expedite: speed up
32. subsequent: following
33. fabricate: make
34. terminate: end
35. fluctuate: change
36. verify: confirm

3

Give your sentences a sense of style

Every now and then I see a newspaper article that sticks in my mind. One article quoted a Harvard English professor who complained that most incoming freshmen wrote in "immigrant prose." By that remark, the professor was not making fun of immigrants; he was merely stating that when immigrants first come to America, they are often unfamiliar with English. And when they do write, they follow the rules of grammar very strictly and write very stiffly.

Like immigrants, too, many students don't know how to make words bob and weave and sting. They don't have a sense of rhythm, a knack for varying sentence structure or the ability to capture their audience. Like immigrants, they write in the basic subject-verb, subject-verb format.

Many students lack this command of the English language because they don't read. If you want to improve your writing, read *The New Yorker*, *The Atlantic Monthly*, and *Esquire*. These magazines constantly run well-written essays. Also pick up *The Best Essays of 1994*.

And read poetry. Sadly, very few people I know read poetry. Yet in poetry, writers really play with words, creating images, turning them upside down and twisting them around to see what the words can accomplish. Of course, I'm not saying that your next business letter should be written like a poem. Your boss might wonder, and rightly so, what you've been sipping at lunch. But poetry does give you a sense of words and what they can accomplish.

Meanwhile, back to immigrant prose. A lot of business writing is very basic "immigrant prose." The person writing has no sense of the structure of the language and no idea how sentences can be varied to make the prose more interesting, to entice, charm and involve the reader. Various techniques, easily learned, can help evolving writers escape the "immigrant prose" syndrome.

Let's look at a few:

Quality of sound

After you've written something, read it out loud. You might wince at the way it sounds. It might grate on your ears. The same thing happens to your readers. When they read it, their subconscious says, "Boy, this is irritating. I just don't like the way this person writes."

Now a letter's quality of sound, the way it reads, is a very subtle thing. Often, to achieve a pleasing sound, you should avoid groups of consonants that just sound rough. For example, read this out loud: "Propelled by the repeated and seemingly needlessly brutal remarks and jabs of the detectives...."

Ow! That made my ears hurt. There is no flow to the sentence. When you read it aloud, you are throwing one harsh sound after another at your reader. Notice, also, that when you read it aloud, it almost reads like a tongue twister. Reading aloud is a way to find how rough your writing style is. If it sounds awkward, it's time to go back and recast the sentence.

One way to make your prose less painful is to use *alliteration*, the repetition of sound to create a special emphasis or rhythm. For example, "the shadow and *h*ush of the *h*aunted past." Or "the *w*ear and *w*aste of *w*estern life." Or "many *ex*perts are already *ex*pecting us..."

Another technique to make your writing less grating is *assonance*, similar vowel sounds. For example, "a perfume esc*a*ped on the g*a*le."

By the way, if you use alliteration or assonance in every sentence, you will drive your readers crazy. Like many writing techniques, use them sparingly to smooth out a sentence or make a letter less grating.

I've got rhythm

When I mention that prose has a distinct rhythm, people often look at me like I'm nuts. (Come to think of it, they look at me that way no matter what I say.)

Every good writer knows that a piece of writing has a sense of rhythm. This rhythm, created by stressing different words and sounds, became very clear to me when I started my job as a speechwriter. A good speech, like a good letter, depends on a good sense of rhythm.

Of course, you don't want the same rhythm flowing throughout an entire letter. Knowing what syllables to stress—and even when to stop a sentence—takes skill.

For example, note this sentence:

While thousands of these jobs are held by high school students looking for gas and movie money, many more are held by people who depend on the paychecks for rent, food and clothes for themselves and their children.

That last phrase, "for themselves and their children," makes the sentence end with a thud. Read the sentence without that thudding phrase attached:

While thousands of these jobs are held by high school students looking for gas and movie money, many more are held by people who depend on the paychecks for rent, food and clothes.

Here's an example of awkward rhythm:

Each company promises before they hire you to pay you more and more, but what happens after you are hired?

A writer with a sense of rhythm would turn this sentence into:

Before you're hired, each corporation promises to pay you more and more. When you're hired, they don't.

Notice how the two sentences are now balanced. One begins with "Before you're hired." The second begins with "When you're hired." These two phrases balance each other out and give the entire statement a flow. Before we broke the sentence apart, we had one long, tongue-twister of a sentence.

A number of factors are behind rhythm. Sometimes simply varying your sentence structure improves the rhythm of a paragraph. In this example, note how John Dos Passos combines both long and short sentences.

Dave Beck was hurt. Dave Beck was indignant. He took the Fifth Amendment when he was questioned and was forced off the executive board of the AFL-CIO, but he retained enough control of his own union treasury to hire a stockade of lawyers to protect him. Prosecution dragged in the courts. Convictions were appealed. Delay.

To give you a better sense of rhythm, let's look at Abraham Lincoln's First Inaugural Address. Secretary of State William Seward thought it needed more of a flourish. But notice that sometimes too much rhetoric can be the wrong cure. Seward showed Lincoln a new draft, which Lincoln rewrote. Note Lincoln's subtle changes that make all the difference in rhythm.

Seward	**Lincoln**
I close.	I am loth to close.
We are not, we must not be, aliens or enemies, but fellow country men and brethren.	We are not enemies, but friends. We must not be enemies
Although passion has strained our bonds of affection too hardly, they must not, I am sure they will not, be broken.	Though passion may have strained, it must not break our bonds of affection.
The mystic chords which, proceeding from so many battlefields and so many patriot graves, pass through all the hearts and hearths in this broad continent of ours, will yet again harmonize all the hearts and hearths in this broad continent of ours, will yet again harmonize in their ancient music when breathed upon by the guardian angel of the nation.	The mystic chords of memory, stretching from every battlefield, and patriot grave, to every living heart and hearth-stone, all over this broad land will yet swell the chorus of all the Union, when again touched, as surely they will be, by the better angels of our nature.

Following are some examples of rhythm. The last example is an excerpt from a speech I wrote for a Presidential candidate. Read the first aloud. Read only portions of the last one aloud. (I can't be that cruel to make anyone read an entire political speech.) All are intended to give you a better feeling for that intangible feeling in prose called rhythm.

Example 1

Walter had just turned the corner of Charles Street into Seventh when he saw her. She was standing a little way up the block talking to a fellow in a black overcoat and a black felt hat, and just the way they were standing—the fellow leaning back against the wall of the building there and she crowded close against him, looking up at him—was enough to make Walter know the kind of talk they were having. Almost without thinking, he stopped and stepped back a pace down Charles, out of sight round the corner.

Example 2

For one brief moment the world was nothing but sea—the sight, the sound, the smell, the touch, the taste of sea.

Example 3

Before we get into this example, I should explain that Ernest Hemingway wrote it. A lot of people try to copy Hemingway by stringing a series of short sentences together. But Hemingway's short sentences aren't what make his writing distinctive. His sense of rhythm sets his writing apart.

We came up on the railway beyond the canal. It went straight toward the town across the low fields. We could see the line of the other railway ahead of us.

Example 4

For everything there is a season, and a time to every purpose under heaven:

a time to be born, and a time to die; a time to plant, and a time to pluck up that which is planted:

a time to kill, and a time to heal; a time to break down, and a time to build up;

a time to weep, and a time to laugh; a time to mourn, and a time to dance;

a time to cast away stones; and a time to gather stones together; a time to embrace, and a time to refrain from embracing;

a time to seek, and a time to lose; a time to keep, and a time to cast away;

a time to rend, and a time to sew; a time to keep silence, and a time to speak;

a time to love, and a time to hate; a time for war, and a time for peace.

—Ecclesiastes

Example 5

American business needs an ethics of fairness

I meet people every day who have drawn their conclusions about "Reaganomics."

But I contend that a conclusion is merely the point where people grew tired of thinking.

I admit it's difficult to think clearly about the Republican's economic policies. A web of illusion spun by the Great Communicator has covered reality. But we must view Reaganomics realistically because realism is the most important ingredient of sound public policy.

We cannot take a shortcut through the facts; we can no longer play Economics in Wonderland.

When we are asked, "Are you better off than you were four years ago?" the American worker must stand up and say, "No!"

Four years ago we hoped that the partial rejuvenation of business would benefit the worker—the worker who shoulders the true economic load of our country. But workers have been left out of the economic renaissance. In fact, the American worker has been taking it on the chin.

The American worker is entering the twenty-first century with his or her sights set low. The hope of owning a home with the two-car garage is receding. The traditional hope of being better off than one's parents has died among many baby boomers. We must look beyond the Yuppies to the Yuffies. The Young Urban Failures.

For every 25-year-old you read about making $300,000 on Wall Street, there are hundreds of 25-year-olds working as fast-food cooks or hospital orderlies earning $3.50 an hour. The rate of home ownership among people under 35 has fallen to 39 percent from 43 percent in 1981.

Americans are struggling to fight off downward mobility. Average weekly earnings, adjusted for inflation, have declined over 14 percent since 1973. Median household income, which was about $26,433 in 1984, has dipped about 8 percent since 1973.

A man who was 30 in 1949 saw his earnings, correct for inflation, rise by 63 percent by the time he turned 40. But a man who was 30 in 1973 saw his real earnings decline by 1 percent by the time he hit 40.

Moonlighting at extra jobs is popular. More married women with children are working than ever before. With their income failing to keep pace with their expectations, Americans are willing to pledge their paychecks to credit cards and don't complain about 18-percent interest. If this is what Reaganomics has driven us to, I say it is time to stop the car and map a new highway.

We need to discover an economy where a father does not have to work two jobs. An economy where he can come home at five o'clock and be with his wife and kids. We need to discover a new economy where a mother is not forced to go to work just to make the car payments. She should have the option of staying home and raising her family if she wishes or working a job where she is fairly compensated for her labor.

Unfortunately for the average American, the future does not look brighter. Many union workers have lost their cost-of-living adjustments. In fact many unions have accepted pay cuts—almost ensuring that their workers had better be working two jobs just to pay the bills.

Talk to any economist. He or she will point out that many of the manufacturing jobs that once catapulted people up the income ladder have been lost to foreign competition.

The $15-an-hour manufacturing job is no more than a dream to our young workers today. In its place, they must settle for minimum wage jobs in *the service sector. Instead of building cars, they are cooking hamburgers; instead of forging steel, they are folding laundry. This is not a future for our young people.*

Reaganomics is not working. The illusion of Reaganomics is working only because people don't want to throw the towel in on the American dream. The fact is consumers are spending more than they can afford. They are living in an economic Disneyland. And when the gates close on the economic Disneyland—when the American family is finally forced to cut back, to pay off the debts they have accumulated, we will be facing a tough period with harsh political and social overtones.

There will be a political backlash like we have never seen before when the economic truth hits home. The class resentment of the 1930s will resurface. How do we prevent this backlash? Well, some people are saying don't panic. There is no emergency yet. But the emergency doesn't start when a man hits the ground. It starts when he falls out of the window. And right now the average American worker is falling out of the window.

Everywhere the American worker turns, he or she is told the solution to our economic dilemma is lower wages.

How do we solve the problem of deregulation? How do businesses become more competitive? Lower wages. And this constant demand for lower wages is hitting baby boomers the hardest.

Two-tiered union contracts pay new workers less than experienced ones. Industry is pushing to hire part-time and temporary workers. The average worker is running twice as fast just to stay in the same place while he or she watches management gain economic ground.

For instance, in the automobile industry the compensation of production workers has risen 32.5 percent during the past five years. But during those same five years, the compensation of top executives has risen by 24.6 percent. We cannot have a petrified order. We cannot say the solution to our economic woes is decreasing wages for an increasing number of Americans.

We must resurrect that concern for equality on a local and national scale if we want to bring the American worker back to his or her rightful place in the world. Business must stop pushing workers to take wage cuts; instead, it must start pushing for fair solutions to the economic problems that affect all of us.

A new kind of force must be created. And that economic force must be molded by fairness. People who work in good faith must be treated in good faith.

Labor does not have to take it on the chin. The average worker does not have to take a pay cut or see a buddy get laid off. There are other avenues, avenues of cooperation that must be explored.

For example, General Motors kept a plant open in Tuscaloosa, Alabama by cutting labor costs, working with labor to reduce overall costs by $2 million a year. A joint task team, composed of labor and management, concentrated on non-labor intensive areas like transportation, energy, inventories and paperwork.

For instance, the task team recommended that warehouses not be air conditioned. You don't need air conditioning to store carburetor parts. That recommendation saved almost $30,000 a year. Instead of piping water into the plant, they tapped an aquifer under the plant. That saved over $70,000 a year.

That spirit of fairness, in which labor was not forced to keep retreating, was created in an atmosphere of trust. And this atmosphere of trust must be extended to a national and international level. We must restore a contract of fairness between labor, management and the government.

No longer can business view government from behind a mask of suspicion. No longer can government arbitrarily implement rules and regulations that shackle business. No longer can we operate in a spirit of confrontation. We must foster a spirit of cooperation with our economic allies.

That same spirit of fairness they forged in a auto plant in Alabama must be carried forth throughout America and throughout the world.

We must unclog our economic thinking. We need no new policies. We must work at a more fundamental level. We must work to ensure that any economic policy is grounded in fairness, and everybody rises with the economic tide. A fair economic policy is not "What can I get away with?" A fair economic policy is "Would I like this deal if I were the receiving end?"

We can't ask what's fair for management. We can't ask what's fair for labor or government. We must ask what is fair for everyone.

And once that social contract of fairness is established, maybe the American worker can truly say, "Yes, I am better off now than I was four years ago." We will stop seeing American jobs shipped overseas. We will turn this economic erosion around. But first we must establish the ground rules. And these ground rules must be ground rules of fairness.

These ground rules must state that business's purpose is not to widen the gap between the salaries of labor and management. Business's purpose is not to eliminate jobs; rather it is to add jobs to our economy.

Only then will we have a politics of progression, not regression. And that is all the American worker wants. A chance to progress.

Thank you!

Okay, so your computer thinks it knows rhythm

Rhythm in writing is something you develop. It's something you know, after years of writing and reading. Rhythm is one of those intangibles that make you a better writer. No computer program can teach you rhythm.

In fact, just for fun, *U.S. News and World Report* once showed how a computer program analyzed the Gettysburg Address:

Eighty-seven	Four score and seven years ago our fathers brought forth on this
Long sentence	continent a new nation, conceived in liberty, and dedicated to the
Passive voice	proposition that all men are created equal.
Passive voice **Is "great" justified?**	Now we are engaged in a great civil war, testing whether that nation, or any nation so conceived and so dedicated, can long endure.
Passive voice	We are met on a great battlefield of that war. We have come to
Long sentence	dedicate a portion of that field as a final resting-place for those
Repeated word	who here gave their lives that that nation might live. It is altogether fitting and proper that we should do this.
Sentence begins with "But"	But, in a larger sense, we cannot dedicate—we cannot
Is sentence too negative?	consecrate—we cannot hallow—this ground. The brave men, living and dead, who struggled here, have consecrated it far above our poor power to add or detract.
Negative	The world will little note, nor long remember, what we say here,
Long sentence	but it can never forget what they did here. It is for us the living,
Passive voice	dedicated here to the unfinished work which they who fought here have thus far so nobly advanced.
Weak start **Passive voice** **Is "great" justified?**	It is rather for us to be here dedicated to the great task remaining before us—that from these honored dead we take
Is sentence too negative?	increased devotion to that cause for which they gave the last

	full measure of devotion; that we here highly resolve that these
Long sentence	dead shall not have died in vain; that this nation, under God, shall have a new birth of freedom, and that government of the people, by the people, for the people,
Negative	shall not perish from the earth.

Summary: Scores zero on strength index. Writer should use active voice, shorter sentences, fewer weak phrases, more positive wording. Overly descriptive with many adjectives. Readability good. Readers need tenth-grade education.

Notice the computer was right. "Four score and seven years ago" *is* wordy. "Eighty-seven" *is* a much more efficient way of saying it. But Lincoln was not striving for efficiency. He was trying to honor the dead and motivate an audience. The rhythm of "four score and seven years ago" helps to set the tone, giving the rest of the speech a dramatic impact. As you read on, you will note, again and again, that from a purely technical point the computer is correct. But machines cannot recognize the subtle nuances of language and rhythm, the texture of words and phrases that move and motivate an audience. Remember, as you write, that you are always writing to another human.

Sentences: the workhorses of your writing

How well you write depends to a great extent on how well you can put a sentence together. In this section, we'll go through the various ways to write sentences. The next time you sit down to write a sentence, you'll be so paranoid you're doing it wrong that you'll never pick up a pen again.

Hey, just kidding! You can use many techniques to make your sentences more powerful. Let's look at some of them.

✔ Put the most important element at the end of the sentence.

If you want to emphasize the idea that you applied for credit:

Don't write: We applied for credit on August 5.

Do write: On August 5, we applied for credit.

Let's look at the Bible for another good example of putting the main idea at the end of the sentence. The Bible did not say, "Killing is something thou shalt not do." It said, "Thou shalt not kill."
Look at this sentence:

> *It's four o'clock, and Tracy Bowman is starting to fade, along with the pale afternoon light.*

To reinforce the key idea, this sentence needs major restructuring. It should read:

> *It's four o'clock, and like the pale afternoon light, Tracy Bowman is starting to fade.*

✅ Simple, strong English makes your sentences more powerful.

Don't write: Although our application for credit was denied, we were encouraged to make cash purchases.

Do write: Our application for credit was denied, but we were encouraged to make cash purchases.

✅ Use short dramatic sentences.

Don't write: To be effective, you cannot revise dogmas; you must smash them.

Do write: You do not revise dogmas. You smash them.

✅ Whenever possible, put in a name.

Don't write: A touchdown was scored in the fourth quarter.

Do write: Ted scored a touchdown in the fourth quarter.

✅ Be specific.

Don't write: Congratulations on your recent honor.
Do write: Congratulations on receiving the Top Sales Award.

Don't write: Thanks for letting us know about your condition.
Do write: Sorry to hear that you broke your leg skiing and that you'll be in a cast for 10 weeks.

Remember this great George Orwell example about being specific. Orwell rewrote this passage from Ecclesiastes (in British bureaucratic fashion):

> *I returned and saw under the sun, that the race is not to the swift, nor the battle to the strong, neither yet bread to the wise, nor yet riches to men of understanding, nor yet favor to men of skill; but time and chance happeneth to them all.*

Now here is Orwell's weakened passage:

> *Objective consideration of contemporary phenomena compels the conclusion that success or failure in competitive activities exhibits no tendency to be commensurate with innate capacity, but that a considerable element of the unpredictable must inevitably be taken into account.*

An interesting point here: When I am hosting a writing seminar, I always tell the class to be specific. They sit there and nod their heads. I then give them a pop quiz by writing this sentence on the board: *Bad weather caused sales to drop.* Then I ask them what is wrong with it. Thankfully, one of the students has listened to me and she says, "It tells me nothing."

I encourage her to go on. She says, "It doesn't say what sales dropped, how far they dropped, what type of bad weather it was...."

And that student is right. If you are going to take the time to put a sentence on a piece of paper, make sure it says something. A sentence that says *A month of rainy weather caused suntan lotion sales to drop by 15 percent in the first quarter* takes up just a little more space than *Bad weather caused sales to drop.* And the more specific example actually gives your reader what he wants—specific information.

✔ Be personal.

Don't write: When people enjoy staying with us, they often fill out a comment card.

Do write: If you enjoyed staying with us, please fill out a comment card.

The point is you are not talking to some abstract entity when you write. You are talking to a real person and the use of the pronoun "you" gives your style a nice personal touch.

☑ **Be positive, not negative.**

Don't write: I will not help you prepare your sales pitch.
Do write: I wish I could help you with your sales pitch.

Don't write: Our store was not closed.
Do write: Our store was open.

☑ **Dashes make your points more emphatic—so do colons.**

Weak: We have a primary need, cash.
Stronger: We have a primary need: cash.

Weak: You are not allowed to make one thing, excuses.
Stronger: You are not allowed to make one thing—excuses.

☑ **Use bullets—they make items stand out.**

Weak: Visa Gold offers everything you want in a credit card including a 9.9 percent rate, no annual fee, an immediate cash advance, no transaction fees...

Strong: Visa Gold has everything you need in a credit card:
- 9.9 percent rate
- No annual fee
- Immediate cash advance
- No transaction fees

☑ **Eliminate *there is* and *there are*.**

Don't write: There are many brave people who traveled the Oregon Trail.
Simply write: Many brave people traveled the Oregon Trail.

☑ **Don't use the passive voice.**

Make your subject do the acting. Make your subject be active, not passive.

Don't say: The ball was hit by John.
Do say: John hit the ball.

Consider this: What if they had written the Bible in passive voice?

In the beginning, the heaven and earth were created by God.

Let's face it, *In the beginning, God created the heaven and earth* is much more powerful and direct.

Or consider how this sentence can be helped by using the active instead of the passive voice:

Cost overruns were incurred by the failure of insufficient oversight.

What they're really trying to say in this sentence is:

The company spent too much money because no one was watching the budget closely.

✔ Watch your adverbs.

Always check your adverbs in a sentence. I'll make you a bet that nine out of 10 times, they aren't needed. Let's look at some quick examples:

She is currently living in New York. It's better to say, *She is living in New York.*

He is clearly incompetent. Excuse me, but what's the difference between *clearly incompetent* and *incompetent*? What's wrong with simply saying *He's incompetent*?

His income increased significantly. Adding *significantly* doesn't do anything for this sentence. Give me the numbers instead. Did his income increase 10 percent? 20 percent? Also, what may be a significant increase to me may be insignificant to you.

Bob is also going. What's wrong with *Bob is going*?

As writer William Zinsser once pointed out, "...totally flabbergasted, I can't imagine anyone being partly flabbergasted, any more than a woman being totally pregnant."

✔ Watch those adjectives.

Mark Twain once said, "Thunder is good, thunder is impressive, but it is lightning that does all the work."

The same is true for words. Nouns and verbs do all the work. Write with nouns and verbs; use adjectives rarely.

Mark Twain had another great quote about adjectives that backs up this point. He once wrote to a schoolboy:

> *I notice that you use plain language, short words and brief sentences. This is the way to write English—it is the modern way and the best way. Stick to it; don't let fluff and flower and verbosity creep in. When you catch adjectives, kill most of them—then the rest will be valuable. An adjective habit or a wordy, diffuse or flowery habit, once fastened upon a person, is as hard to get rid of as any other vice.*

Mark Twain also said, "As to the adjective, when in doubt, strike it out."

✔ We know, we know...please spare us!

Don't state the obvious. Don't say "blue in color," "five in number," "square in shape," "the landscaping of the grounds," "the architecture of the building."

✔ Don't be redundant.

Closely related to the use of too many adverbs and adjectives is a sin covered by the strange word *pleonasm*. *Pleonasms* are phrases that say the same thing twice.

Some examples:

hot water heater	first things first
cold ice	small speck
sharp point	female hen
round circle	hard cement
empty vacuum	poor beggar
dark black	lethal bullets
major masterpiece	fast jet
lazy bum	round wheel
final conclusion	first-year freshman
three-cornered triangle	wealthy millionaire
three-point field goal	dirty cesspool
woman pregnant with child	dead corpse

My final conclusion is, don't use pleonasms.

More tips on improving sentence structure

☑ Inverted style

Inverted sentence order can be a good way to achieve variety in your sentences.

This job he kept six years.
Then came the greatest upset of all.
And in one corner, looking out of place among the over-dressed guests, stood Kathleen.

Note that too many inverted sentences can be a bit much, and you could be subjected to the same criticism leveled at *Time* magazine's writing style: "Backwards ran the sentences until reeled the mind."

☑ Parallelism

Parallelism means using the same construction or building techniques throughout the entire sentence.

Health insurance will be provided *to help* employees *to eliminate* fear of high medical bills and *to show* what a great company this is.

Did you notice that all three reasons for providing health insurance are constructed the same way—to help, to eliminate and to show. The sentence would have had a parallelism problem if we had written it this way: Health insurance will be provided for *helping employees, solving high medical costs* and *to show what* a great company this is.

Parallelism helps give your instructions a continuity and makes them easier to follow.

Let's look at another example of nonexistent parallel construction:

The instructions are as follows: First, plug in the cord. The next thing is that the power is turned on. The videotape then should be inserted and made sure it is rewound. Then you can push play, while ignoring the clock blinking 12:00.

Notice how much easier these instructions are to follow when parallel construction is used:

The instructions are as follows: First, plug the cord in. Next, turn the power on. Then insert a videotape and check to see that it has been rewound. Finally, push play. Ignore the blinking clock. Only your 10-year-old can stop it from blinking, but he will demand a big hike in his allowance.

☑ The long and short of it

Hello, my name is Phil. I live in Phoenix. It is a big city. I like the city. Phoenix is in Arizona.

Wasn't that last paragraph exciting? Notice that each sentence was four or five words long. There's nothing wrong with five-word sentences. But string a bunch of them together and they will be selling your letters as sleeping tonics. Variety is the spice of life, especially when it comes to sentence structure.

The writer Gary Provost explained how sentences vary this way:

"The ear demands variety. Now listen. I vary the sentence length, and I create music. Music. The writing sings. It has a pleasant rhythm, a harmony. I use short sentences. And I use sentences of medium length. And sometimes when I am certain the reader is rested, I will engage him with a sentence of considerable length, a sentence that burns with energy and builds with all the impetus of a crescendo, the roll of the drums, the crash of the cymbals—sounds that say listen to this, it is important."

☑ Fragment

And there's a simple answer to the complexity of George Thomas. What is he really like? Stiff. Uncompromising. Effective.

☑ Periodic sentence

A periodic sentence builds to a strong conclusion. It completes its main thought at the end. You make the reader wait until the end of the sentence for the full meaning or significance to emerge.

If you really want to show some initiative, to market your own ideas in your own way, then don't work for a large corporation.

That John Dillinger was only an accomplice seems certain.

Though we seek the easy way, hope to win the lottery or hope to get a big check in the mail, only hard work will pay our bills.

 Isolation

A word or phrase is isolated by punctuation. In the following example, notice how the name Theibert is isolated from the rest of the sentence by the phrase, "it was often said." This technique, called isolation, separates the name and makes it stand out.

Theibert, it was often said, was the last to know anything.

Isolating words or phrases at both ends of a sentence is also possible. Note how this sentence by Dylan Thomas isolates and emphasizes both "position" and "difficult."

The position—if poets must have positions, other than upright—of the poet born in Wales or of Welsh parentage and writing his poems in English is today made by many people unnecessarily, and trivially, difficult.

You can also isolate a word or phrase in the middle of a sentence.

Our sales figures—and there's no excuse—are down for the first quarter.

Repetition

Sometimes it does not hurt to repeat your point. You don't want to do it too often, but repetition of the word or phrase can help hammer your point home.

I didn't like the accounting class; I didn't like accounting; I didn't like the accounting teacher, and after all these years, I still don't.

Problem gives rise to problem.

Verbs

You write with nouns and verbs. Especially with verbs. Verbs denote action. Nothing more, nothing less. If you use weak verbs, your writing just lies there, begging for someone to put it out of its misery. If you use strong verbs, your writing comes alive. It gets up and struts around the reader's mind, making a lasting impression.

If you remember anything from this book, remember this: The best way to improve your writing? Write with powerful verbs that hammer your point home. If you want wimpy writing, don't read this section. It will tell you how to supercharge your writing style through the strength of verbs!

Let's get cracking.

✔ Use a verb!

Often the best way to clean up a sentence, to make it strong and direct, is to use a verb. The use of just one verb eliminates unnecessary words and makes the prose move quickly, propelling your reader along.

For example, we could say, "The snow, like a blanket, covered the countryside." But let's take the word "blanket" and make it into a verb. The sentence now reads: "Snow blanketed the countryside."

This skill, replacing a phrase with a verb, is especially useful in business communications. Again, look at this example:

They made a decision to hire Jones.

Let's replace the phrase "made a decision" with one word—*decided*. The sentence now reads:

They decided to hire Jones.

If you want even better editing, let's get rid of "decided." The sentence now reads:

They hired Jones.

A short, powerful sentence. And all because we use one good verb in the place of three or four so-so words. More examples follow.

Don't write: He took action on the Jones account.
Do write: He acted on the Jones account.

Don't write: He submitted an argument that Jones should
            be kept on staff.
Do write: He argued that Jones should be kept on staff.

Don't write: It is the company's intention to review the
            Jones case.
Do write: The company will review the Jones case.

Don't write: He offered an explanation on the firing of Jones.

Do write: He explained why he fired Jones.

Don't write: Jones could have achieved dominance in the industry.

Do write: Jones could have dominated the industry.

Don't write: Jones and the company came to an agreement.

Do write: Jones and the company agreed.

Don't write: By firing Jones, the company realized a savings of big bucks.

Do write: By firing Jones, the company saved big bucks.

Don't write: By firing Jones, the company is in violation of the Americans with Disabilities Act.

Do write: By firing Jones, the company violated the Americans with Disabilities Act.

Don't write: Jones's contention was that he was fired because he was vertically impaired.

Do write: Jones contended he was fired because he was vertically impaired. (That's "short" to us common folks.)

Don't write: The company finally reached a finding on the Jones case.

Do write: The company found Jones was right.

Don't write: The company gave consideration to rehiring vertically impaired Jones.

Do write: The company considered rehiring Jones.

Don't write: The company's attorneys provided information on what Jones did.

Do write: The company's attorneys claimed Jones embezzled $100,000. (Note the combination of a stronger verb and a specific statement.)

> *Don't write*: Jones's attorney assessed the information and determined it was wrong.
>
> *Do write*: Jones's attorney determined the information was wrong.

> *Don't write*: The company made a decision to make a payment of $10,000 to Jones.
>
> *Do write*: The company decided to pay Jones $10,000.

> *Don't write*: After the verdict, Jones went out and had a collision with the truck.
>
> *Do write:* After the verdict, a truck smashed into Jones.

> *Don't write*: I must make the assumption that Jones was having a tough day.
>
> *Do write*: I assume Jones was having a tough day.

That's enough. I've had it with the story of Jones. I draw the conclusion that it's gone on long enough. Okay, I *conclude* it's gone on long enough.

✔ Use strong verbs

The writer Theodore Bernstein makes a strong case for strong verbs. He once noted that the authors of the Declaration of Independence needed to achieve two goals: to justify the colonists' claim to independence, plus they had to spur them into action. They achieved this by using strong, powerful words. Bernstein pointed out that the constant use of strong verbs ("King George III has plundered our seas, ravished our coasts, burned our towns and destroyed the lives of our people") truly makes the Declaration of Independence a powerful call to action.

In short, your writing is only as strong as the verbs you use. When you write something, go through it and circle every time you use *is* or *have* or a form of the verb *to be*. Then try to replace these with stronger verbs.

For example: Bob *is* going *to be* at the meeting, and he *is* taking notes, which he *will be* presenting to us when he *is* back in town.

Rewrite the sentence as: After Bob takes notes at the meeting, he'll fly back to Phoenix and present them to us.

Look at the difference between the following two paragraphs. Note the use of weak versus strong verbs.

When Mr. Fulton was testing his steamship, a crowd was on the banks. As he was getting the boat going, some of the crowd was saying, "She'll never start." But she was started and she was going down the river when the same people said, "She'll never stop, she'll never stop."

When Mr. Fulton launched his first steamship, a crowd gathered on the bank. As the engine roared, the smoke belched, and the craft shook violently, the crowd shouted, "She'll never start." But off she cruised up the river with the same people—astonished— shouting, "She'll never stop. She'll never stop."

Note how verbs make this paragraph come to life:

"The team grew old. The Dodgers deserted Brooklyn. Wreckers swarmed into Ebbets Field and leveled the stands. Soil that had felt the spikes of Robinson and Reese was washed from the faces of mewling children. The New York Herald Tribune *withered, changed its face and collapsed. I covered a team that no longer exists in a demolished ball park for a newspaper that is dead."*

—Roger Kahn, *The Boys of Summer*

✔ Watch those prepositions

Remember, when in doubt, put in a strong verb. Sometimes people use prepositional phrases instead of verbs. Ugh!

Don't write: Columbus came upon America.
Do write: Columbus discovered America (even if doing so is not politically correct).

Don't write: I can't put up with my kid anymore.
Do write: I can't stand my kid anymore.

Don't write: I took hold of the coffee cup, and upon grasping it, I felt a great heat come upon me.
Do write: I grabbed the coffee cup and burned myself.

☑ **Turn a negative into a positive**

Don't write: I didn't remember my anniversary.

Do write: I'm a dead duck (hey, hey, just kidding).

Do write: I forgot my anniversary.

Watch placement of words those!

Finally, as you strive for that perfect sentence, don't forget to check the placement of your words or phrases. Word order can make a great difference. For example, you could say, "He was *only* the engineer" or you could say, "He was the *only* engineer."

In fact, the following examples from church bulletins show how the wrong word or phrase in the wrong place can cause embarrassment.

This afternoon, there will be a meeting in the south and north ends of the church. Children will be baptized at both ends.

Tuesday at 4 p.m., there will be an ice cream social. All ladies giving milk, please come early.

Wednesday, the Ladies Literary Society will meet. Mrs. Johnson will sing "Put Me in My Little Bed" accompanied by the pastor.

This being Easter Sunday, we will ask Mrs. Johnson to come forward and lay an egg on the altar.

Thursday at 5 p.m., there will be a meeting of the Little Mothers Club. All wishing to become Little Mothers please meet the minister in his study.

The service will close with "Little Drops of Water"...one of the ladies will start quietly and the rest of the congregation will join in.

On Sunday, a special collection will be taken to defray the expenses of the new carpet. All wishing to do something on the carpet, please come forward and get a piece of paper.

The ladies of the church have cast off clothing of every kind and they may be seen in the church basement on Friday afternoon.

This Friday at 7 p.m., there will be a hymn singing in the park across from the church. Bring a blanket and come prepared to Sin.

While amusing in church bulletins, these slip-ups can be embarrassing in the business world. Think how the woman felt who wrote, "I was Chief Financial Officer for a wholesaler of women's slacks. We also sold men's bottoms."

In short, proofread, proofread, proofread!

We have come far together

If you have followed every point thus far, I am impressed. I also bet that if you have put all these tips into practice, you're already a much better writer.

Now for a little review. Read the next part quickly. Enjoy it. I'll join you at the end of it to introduce the next section.

A very short course in writing

Do you make common mistakes that weaken your writing? To put more power into your writing, here are four rules that make the mistakes you shouldn't make: Read these carefully and I know you will find the mistakes. See how smart you are already?

1. Perpetuate perspicuity: idiosyncratically euphemistic eccentricities are the promulgators of triturable obfuscation.

2. Omit words that are needless on the grounds that they clutter up your writing. Most people operate under the belief that using a lot of words affords them the opportunity to communicate better.

3. Don't allow the modification of verbs to result in the formation of nouns. This occurrence usually takes place with the addition of a suffix onto the verb, such as "-tion," "-ment" or "-ence." The problem with this is that it causes the addition of clutter, the impedance of understanding and the loss of power.

4. The active voice of verbs is preferred over the passive voice. In the active voice, the doing or the acting is done by the subject. Your writing is more direct and forceful by using active voice. Wordiness is created by the passive voice because a *helping verb* (*to be* or *to have*) is used with the main verb.

Wow! What did those rules really say? Here's a translation:

1. Keep it simple. Fancy language doesn't clarify, it confuses.
2. Omit needless words. Less is better.
3. Give verbs power. Don't "nounify" them by adding "-tion," "-ence" or "-ment."
4. Use the active voice. Active: *The committee was interested in the idea.* Passive: *Interest in the idea was shown by the committee.*

You're ready to go onto the next section: *Psychology.* At this point, you've learned how to organize your material and how to watch out for the many little things, from clichés to weak verbs, that can destroy your writing.

Now you'll move on to a vital part of your writing "tool kit." No matter how well organized your report is, no matter how perfected your style, your writing must be built on a firm foundation of thought and psychology. By psychology, I mean those techniques that show you understand your audience and know the best methods to communicate with them. Your prose may be a work of art, but you still have to grab your reader's attention and hang onto it.

So let's get started!

Chapter 3 summary

We started this chapter by stating that too many businesspeople write what we call "immigrant prose." Their sentences repeat the same pattern over and over—subject, verb, subject, verb, subject, verb—with all the sentences being about the same length. You must work hard to vary your sentence structure, you must work hard to make your sentences understandable.

Let's close this chapter with two tips. The first is from the writer Richard Lanham and describes how you can ensure that your sentences are not all the same, boring length. He said:

> *"Take a piece of your prose and a red pencil and draw a slash after every sentence. Two or three pages ought to make a large enough sample. If the red marks occur at regular intervals, you have, as they used to say in the White House, a problem. Vary your sentence lengths. Naturally enough, complex patterns will fall into long sentences and emphatic conclusions work well when short. But no rules prevail except to avoid monotony."*

The final tip is from writer Bill Scott. He tells what to do when a sentence stinks:

> *"Change it. How? Easy. Read a stinky sentence over. Figure out what it means. Now...put the sentence's meaning in your own words....You may have to expand the sentence into two or three sentences. That's allowed."*

What shouldn't be allowed are sentences that drone on and on and put your reader to sleep. Write the best sentences you can. They are the backbone of your whole memo, letter or report.

4

The psychology of writing

You can have all the technical details of your report, presentation, letter or memo down, but if you don't consider what's on the minds of your audience, you have wasted your time. People have different concerns, different areas of interest and different problems. To communicate effectively, figure out who you are writing for, what their concerns are, and what they want to know.

Consider these five questions on your reader's mind.

1. What is it?
2. What does it do?
3. What does that mean to me?
4. Who says so besides you?
5. Can you prove it?

Answering these five questions will help you avoid "writer-based" copy. Writer-based copy is written from your point of view. The letter or report should be written from the reader's point of view. Why?

Remember the famous words of Cicero, "Every living creature loves itself."

That translates to: When people read your report, they don't care how brilliant you sound, they want to know what is in it for them. *Remember, each of us thinks about our own interests about 95 percent of the time.*

This short anecdote shows the difference between writer-based and reader-based copy.

During the Revolutionary War, General Braddock needed 150 wagons and horses for a battle campaign. His first advertisement basically said, "We want wagons or else."

Now, that was written from General Edward Braddock's viewpoint, and he only got 25 wagons. Benjamin Franklin rewrote the advertisement to fit the readers' needs, not the writer's needs. His new advertisement contained only one paragraph about *what Braddock wanted* and six numbered paragraphs about *what the farmers would get.* Franklin received more than 100 wagons, enough to meet the army's need.

Talented writers understand Abraham Maslow's five-level hierarchy of needs. Generally speaking, people must have lower-level needs on the hierarchy met before they pursue higher-level needs. The first level includes the basic human needs for survival and sex; the second level, the need for safety and security; the third level, the need for belonging; the fourth level, the need for self-esteem, recognition and competence; and the fifth level, the need for self-actualization, challenge and realization of potential.

This hierarchy of needs explains why many attempts to introduce new corporate cultures fail. Most company communications, when a new culture is introduced, challenge workers to "strive harder," "work smarter" and "seek new challenges."

But these things employees are being urged to do are on the top level of Maslow's hierarchy. Communicators seem to forget that when a new culture or massive change is introduced into an organization, employees are more worried about safety and security, self-esteem and competence to handle the new requirements; all of these are found much lower on Maslow's hierarchy.

You cannot build a communication program that emphasizes the top level while ignoring the foundation formed by the four lower levels. Yet, poor communicators consistently do this.

In short, as you start any piece of writing, remember that you are writing to human beings, all with their own needs, their own insecurities and their own distinctive ways of approaching things. Remember, no matter how "corporate" you want to sound, take time to consider your readers' psychology, what's on their minds, and make an emotional appeal in many of the items you write.

As G.K. Chesterton pointed out:

The world has kept sentimentalities simply because they are the most practical things in the world. They alone make men do things. The world does not encourage a perfectly rational lover, simply because a perfectly rational lover would never get married. The world does not encourage a perfectly rational army, because a perfectly rational army would run away.

Finally, as you begin to write, here are 10 top emotional appeals you should consider using.

1. People think about themselves about 95 percent of the time. So write from their viewpoint, not yours!

2. Don't tell someone you want them *to do* something. Get them *to want* to do it.

3. People don't do things based on *your* values. They do something based on *their* values. Understand the other person's value system.

4. People want to feel better about themselves. How can you help them accomplish this goal?

5. I know it's a cliché, but always try to construct a "win-win" situation. A good "deal" takes place when you would be willing to be on the other end of it.

6. Show the people you're writing for how the solution will make the work easier or help them get promoted.

7. Remember self-esteem is very important to people. How will your idea help people think of themselves as honest, kind, caring and responsible?

8. People want to make a difference. They don't want to shuffle paper. How can you make your readers feel they are doing something that matters?

9. Will the steps you recommend help people avoid failure and future trouble?

10. People want to be noticed; they want to know their opinions make a difference. Will your writing convince readers they will be listened to?

Now it's time to move ahead. The next section will help you understand your audience and learn to employ the right psychology when writing any business correspondence.

Putting the human touch back into your writing

When you're writing a letter, you're writing to another human being. Although that sounds obvious, you may forget it when you are writing.

Don't slip into a "business frame of mind" and produce language devoid of feeling, emotion or even the slightest hint that an actual human wrote it.

Following are two letters. The first was written by a man explaining to his customers that he was taking over his father's business. From the letter you get a sense of pride; the man is proud of his father and the business his father built.

The second letter Charles Dickens wrote to his wife, informing her that their child might soon die. At that time Dickens's wife was also recovering from a severe illness. This letter shows the gentle and powerful use of language. Although I doubt you would use it as a model for a business letter, it is a good example to remind you that you are always one human being writing to another.

Example 1

The history of Consolidated Auto Sales is a story of the dedication and hard work of one man, my father, Roman Sarwark. He moved to Arizona in 1942 on doctor's orders to escape the cold weather. He started selling cars on the corner of 16th Street and Van Buren and has been there ever since.

He has dedicated 53 years of his life to create a successful business and to support his family. I have worked for my father in the family business since 1972. During that time, I have learned all the phases of the business, from repairing cars to buying and selling them. Over the years, I have gradually been taking over duties that were done by my father.

Through this time he has been a guiding hand, making sure that I learn the lessons of his many years of experience well. Now that Roman is 82 years old, he has decided that it is time for me to take over the helm of the company. He will remain as an advisor and mentor.

There will be no change in the way we do business at Consolidated Auto Sales. What we have done over the years has proved to work, for us and for our customers. If anything changes, it will be to give better service and better products to our customers. I believe that after 53 years in business, our company will survive for another 53 years.

In closing, I want to reassure our customers and others we deal with that nothing is going to change. I look forward to seeing each and every one of you again and again. I know we have third-generation customers. I would like to believe that their children will also go on to buy cars from us.

Example 2

Devonshire Terrace
Tuesday morning, 15 April, 1851

My dearest Kate: Now observe, you must read this letter very slowly and carefully. If you have hurried on thus far without quite understanding (apprehending some bad news), I rely on your turning back and reading again.

Little Dora, without being in the least pain, is suddenly stricken ill. There is nothing in her appearance but perfect rest—you would suppose her quietly asleep, but I am sure she is very ill, and I cannot encourage myself with much hope of her recovery. I do not (and why should I say I do to you, my dear?) I do not think her recovery at all likely.

I do not like to leave home. I can do no good here, but I think it right to stay. You would not like to be away, I know, and I cannot reconcile it to myself to keep you away. Forster, with his usual affection for us, comes down to bring you this letter and to bring you home, but I cannot close it without putting the strongest entreaty and injunction upon you to come with perfect composure— to remember what I have often told you, that we can never expect to be exempt, as to our children, from the afflictions of other parents, and that when you come I should have to say to you, "Our little baby is dead," you are to do your duty to the rest, and to show yourself worthy of the great trust you hold in them.

If you will only read this steadily, I have a perfect confidence in your doing what is right.

Ever affectionately,

Charles Dickens

Now after those two examples, let's look at a typical business letter.

Dear Mr. Perez:

After receiving your inquiry, we launched an investigation as to the whereabouts of your recent payment. You did remit your payment as required, and our investigation showed we had posted it to the wrong account. We hope that this has not inconvenienced you greatly, and we will post the amount to the right balance.

That letter is about as friendly as a dark alley in New York. The writer did not treat Mr. Perez as a human being; he treated him like... well, even I'm not sure who deserves that kind of cold response.

The sad part is that it doesn't take much more time or energy to write in a friendly manner. Why couldn't this writer have sent Mr. Perez a letter like the following?

> *Dear Mr. Perez:*
>
> *Whoops! Our mistake. You paid, and we messed up by posting the check to the wrong account. We have corrected the mistake, and please accept my personal assurance it won't happen again.*
>
> *Meanwhile, I know it took a lot of time on your part to help us straighten out this mess. So I've enclosed two free movie tickets. I know that won't pay for your time, but I send them with hope for a better relationship between us in the future.*
>
> *Thanks!*

Let's look at another letter. It's not that bad but could be much better. What prompted this letter? Mr. Sanchez's wife cannot read English. And sometimes, by mistake, his wife pays the gas bill instead of the electric bill. So Mr. Sanchez has written to the CEO of the local utility suggesting that a little light bulb symbol be put at the top of the bill so his wife will know it's the electric bill.

Now remember, Mr. Sanchez has written his letter in very basic English. He does not have a firm grasp of English either. In fact, here is an excerpt from his letter:

> *It goes these way—my wife does not talk English, but she does keep on eye on things of the house....*

The utility sent Mr. Sanchez this response:

> *Dear Mr. Sanchez:*
>
> *Thank you for taking the time to write to me with your suggestion of having a symbol on our bills for easier identification by our customers.*
>
> *Your letter emphasizes the need for our utility as we transcend within our organization, to consistently strive to improve the methodology in which we communicate with our customers. To this end, we are offering much of our collateral material in Spanish, and we also have a language bank to assist customers who cannot speak English.*

We are presently in the process of evaluating and revising our billing format, and I have asked the personnel involved to consider your proposal. I have also forwarded your suggestion to our Communications and Publications departments to investigate the possibility of employing more symbols in the collateral materials we produce.

Again, I appreciate your input in helping us do a better job of servicing you.

Sincerely,

Reader participation

Here is what I think is wrong with the letter:

_____
_____
_____
_____
_____
_____
_____
_____
_____
_____
_____
_____
_____
_____
_____

Okay, let's quickly list some of this letter's problems:

Stilted bureaucratic language: "I have asked the personnel involved to consider your proposal." This could be written in plain English. "I had my billing employees read your letter."

Weak nouns: "I appreciate your *input*." Again, simply say, "Thanks for writing."

Mysterious terms: What is a "language bank"? Can you make deposits and withdrawals?

Oh no, an "-ology" word: This guy can barely understand English, and we're throwing "methodology" at him. "Methods" would be bad enough. Why don't they replace the word "methodology" with the simple word "way?"

Not walking the talk: The letter says the utility has a language bank. Why not use it and send him a letter back in Spanish? Then his wife can read it, too.

Not calling a spade a spade: "Collateral material"? Come on. Call them "newsletters" or "brochures" or "fliers."

This list covers only some of the basic problems in the letter and many business letters like it. How could the letter be rewritten to treat Mr. Sanchez like a human being? Here's one option.

Dear Mr. Sanchez:

Thank you for your great idea. Beginning next month, we will put a little light bulb at the top of our bills. If you have any more good ideas for us, please write again. And, once more, thanks!

As you review the Sanchez letter, please remember this important point: The words you use must be tailored to your reader. Plus, the words you use can make or fail to make a connection.

Ethos, pathos and logos

More than 2,000 years ago, Aristotle described the three traits necessary to be a persuasive speaker. These traits apply equally well to writing. The first trait is *ethos*. A rough translation of "ethos" is "credibility." Your reader must be willing to believe you before he or she will be convinced of anything.

In fact, much of the political gridlock in America occurs because voters no longer believe in the credibility of many of their elected officials. Thus, it is difficult for politicians to convince voters of new ideas. Or look at it this way: Say you are choosing a surgeon to operate on you, you are selecting a general to lead you into battle, or you are selecting a teacher for your child. As you make such important decisions, that person's credibility is one of the top things you consider. Don't think that your credibility as a writer is not crucial. Often your words, put on paper forever, are what people will judge you by.

I have often found that when I am selling an article to *The Wall Street Journal* or another publication, one of the most important things I can do up front is establish my credibility. For example, an article I wrote on speechwriting started out, "I have been a speechwriter for more than 10 years."

Another article began, " 'You cannot bore people into buying.' The years I spent writing direct-mail copy drilled that classic David Ogilvy line into my head..." Again, right up front I established my credibility.

This story shows how important credibility is in speaking (or in writing):

Scheduled to speak in Philadelphia at the Town Hall, Bishop Fulton J. Sheen decided to walk from his hotel even though he was unfamiliar with the city. Sure enough, he became lost and was forced to ask some boys to direct him to his destination. One boy asked Sheen, "What are you going to do there?"

"I'm going to give a lecture," replied the Bishop.

"About what?"

"On how to get to heaven. Would you care to come along?"

"Are you kidding?" said the boy, "You don't even know how to get to Town Hall!"

One more story about credibility:

It was the big sales meeting. The sales manager and his sales reps were discussing their product, a kids' cereal.

Winding up the meeting, the sales manager shouted, "Who's got the best company in the United States?" and the sales people yelled back, "We do!"

"And who's got the best advertising in the United States?" Again came the same reply.

"And who's got the best toys in their cereal?" The sales people yelled again, "We do!"

"Then why can't we sell more cereal?" the sales manager demanded.

"Maybe," piped up a saleswoman in the front row, "the kids don't like it."

The second, and perhaps most important, of Aristotle's three ways to persuade people, is *pathos*. Aristotle believed that unless you could move your audience through pathos, or emotional appeals, persuading them to change their beliefs or take action would be difficult.

Modern advertising is based entirely on Aristotle's trait of pathos. Every copywriter worth his or her salt realizes that people decide to act based on their emotions. Face it, no one ever buys a new car based on logic alone. The emotional appeal of a new car, what you think it says about you, its smell, the new car showroom—none of these is a logical appeal. They are appeals based on pure emotion.

Consider the most important decisions you've made in your life ranging from choosing a good friend to finding a mate, from buying a house to
choosing a vocation. You made these big decisions based on emotion.

Perhaps e.e. cummings said it best when he explained in a poem that
"feeling is first":

> *since feeling is first*
> *who pays any attention*
> *to the syntax of things*
> *will never wholly kiss you;*
> *wholly to be a fool*
> *while Spring is in the world*
> *my blood approves,*
> *and kisses are a better fate than wisdom*
> *lady I swear by all flowers. Don't cry*
> *the best gesture of my brain is less than*
> *your eyelids flutter which says*
> *we are for each other: then*
> *laugh, leaning back in my arms*
> *for life's not a paragraph*
> *And death i think is no parenthesis*

The point is, emotion sells. In fact, the best way to grab an audience
in a speech or presentation is to bring some emotion to your speech. Rufus
K. Broadway, M.D., told the West Virginia Medical Association about the
heartbreaking decision he once had to make:

> *"This was when the government was just starting to consider*
> *whether kidney dialysis should be funded in renal failure cases.*
> *The government set up some pilot programs, but the funds were so*
> *limited they had to set up committees to decide who would be*
> *dialyzed. And I was on the first committee in Miami. One evening*
> *we met to choose between two young patients—because we could*
> *only dialyze one of them. One was a working man with a wife and*
> *three children, and the other was a lovely 16-year-old girl who was*
> *destined to become a concert pianist. One would live. And the other*
> *would die. It was up to us to decide. And I resigned the next*
> *morning because I didn't want to play God."*

The last part of Aristotle's equation deals with *logos*: organization and
logic. Your readers will validate their actions through logic, or logos
(brains). But they will expect you to give them specific facts and figures
that will convince them. Don't just give them generalities. In fact, Aristotle said, "Generalities are the refuge of weak minds."

Using facts and figures with a little emotion attached is better yet. This technique is perhaps best demonstrated by the story told about L.L. Bean (yes, *that* L.L. Bean). During World War II, he was in Washington as a consultant to the armed forces. For cold-weather wear, the army wanted leather-topped rubbers with 16-inch tops. Bean thought 12-inch tops and a lighter rubber would be better.

Getting nowhere with verbal argument, he whipped out a pencil and began calculating. "Gentlemen," he said, "do you realize that if you insist on the higher-topped boot, in a day's march of 36,980 steps each soldier in the Army will be lifting 4,600 unnecessary pounds?"

The Army bought his logic. And notice how neatly L.L. Bean packaged logic and emotion together.

Can you analyze the psychology in this letter?

A few years ago, the Hertz Coorporation had a dishonest employee who could have caused a major public relations headache. But notice how Hertz executives used psychology in this letter to CEOs of major companies across the U.S. to reestablish credibility with customers, to subtly play on customers' emotions and to encourage customers to look toward the future with Hertz. As you read the letter, pick out parts where Hertz used ethos, pathos and logos. Following the letter is my quick analysis.

Dear Mr. / Ms. CEO:

During the past few weeks, The Hertz Corporation has been the subject of news reports concerning the company's accident claims practices prior to 1985. We want you to hear—from us—how and why this practice occurred and to understand that it was corrected three years ago on our own initiative. Although this incident has been highly publicized, the fact remains that we have taken every step to run our company with integrity and to provide the quality and service you expect from Hertz.

During the period in question, Hertz, like many of its competitors, submitted claims for damages to its vehicles at prices based on prevailing rates. (About 30 percent of these claims were against Hertz renters, 70 percent against third parties responsible for the damage.) Because we receive volume discounts from repair shops, however, we did not have to pay the quoted rates for the repairs. Hertz's management was aware of this practice and, on advice of legal counsel, believed all our operations were proper. In fact, if properly documented, this practice would be nothing more than that which is practiced by our competitors today.

Unfortunately, the system was abused by one employee, the national accident control manager. In an overzealous attempt to boost the performance of his division and to enhance his own position in the company, he created illegal and inappropriate procedures that resulted in the submission of claims for damages that were based on false documentation.

When Hertz's management became aware of these irregularities in 1985, we immediately commenced a thorough internal investigation and review of our company's accident claims procedures.

As a result of this investigation, all questionable or illegal practices were stopped, the national accident control manager was fired, and Hertz began a voluntary program to make restitution to all those who may have been overcharged as a result of these practices. To date, Hertz has refunded more than three million dollars.

We also changed our entire billing procedure for vehicle repairs, and our internal reporting structure was revamped to ensure that these practices do not recur.

Most of our competitors, including Avis, still calculate the amount they bill their customers or others responsible for vehicle damage on the estimated retail prices listed in reference manuals. No discounts are passed on.

For almost two years, however, it has been Hertz's policy to submit damage claims for only the amount that we are actually charged by repair shops. In short, Hertz does pass on all discounts we receive.

All of us at Hertz regret that those past practices ever took place and that they evaded detection for so long. When they were discovered, they were thoroughly investigated—by Hertz—and resolved—by Hertz—a year before Hertz became aware of any government investigation into the matter. However, because the government is expected to announce the results of its investigation soon, we expect there will be more publicity about this story.

Going forward, we are committed to providing the best service in the industry, and to proving once again that we are worthy of the confidence you have shown in us since 1918.

Notice that right up front Hertz tried to establish credibility. They used *ethos* when they wrote, "We want you to hear—from us—how and why this practice occurred and to understand that it was corrected three years ago on our own initiative."

Then, once they have established credibility, notice how they move onto *pathos*. Who doesn't have to put up with a dishonest employee now and then? Hertz writes: "Unfortunately, the system was abused by one employee, the national accident control manager. In an overzealous attempt to boost the performance of his division and to enhance his own position in the company...."

Now that Hertz has established credibility and appealed to your emotions, they hit you with *logic*—the cold, hard facts:

> *"For almost two years, however, it has been Hertz's policy to submit damage claims for only the amount that we are actually charged by repair shops. In short, Hertz does pass on all discounts we receive."*

I have only touched upon the *ethos, pathos* and *logos* that Hertz used in the letter. Next time you have to sell an idea, write a compelling letter or memo, don't be afraid to reread the Hertz letter and use the same concepts of *ethos, pathos* and *logos* that they did.

The most effective words to sell ideas

A Yale University study stated that these are the 11 most effective words you can use to persuade readers. They are effective because readers understand them more than any other words in their vocabularies. They are:

• discover	• love	• results
• ease	• money	• save
• guarantee	• new	• you
• health	• proven	

Who, what, where, when, why

Of course you've heard of the five famous W's. They're so famous that there must be a statue dedicated to them at some famous university. Yet, despite knowing the five famous W's, many people don't write them down before writing their document.

Writing down the five famous W's forces you to answer them and gives you a better focus on your topic and a better understanding of your audience.

Who?

- Who will be reading this?
- Who is the main reader?
- Do they know who *you* are?
- Who do you want to take action?
- Who has requested this?
- Who may be screening it?
- Who are the main players the reader must know about?
- Who won't be reading it, so you can leave out certain parts?
- Who will be affected by the action taken?

What?

- What do you want to achieve?
- What are you going to cover?
- What key points must you make?
- What points are okay to leave out and discuss later?
- What action must the reader take?
- What knowledge must the reader have to understand your report?
- What must the reader know about your expertise?
- What is fact and what is opinion?
- What is the next stage of the project?
- What are the options?
- What must be done to avoid loss of sales, customers, etc.?
- What are the reader's motives?
- What are the reader's responsibilities?
- What is the reader's span of control? What can he or she control?
- What questions might the reader have?
- What objections might the reader have?
- What do you expect the reader's response to be?
- What environment is the reader used to working in? Management? Front-line?
- What's in it for the reader?
- What warnings should be included?
- What projections should be included?
- What is the urgency of this?
- What is your conclusion?

Why?

- Why are you writing this?
- Why should the reader care?
- Why should the reader take action?
- Why are certain steps so crucial?
- Why should the reader share this with someone else?
- Why should the reader buy into your conclusions?
- Why should the reader go with your company?
- Why have you reached your conclusion?
- Why do I want to meet with this person?
- Why do I want that interview?
- Why do I want them to buy this product?

Where?

- Where will the actions suggested lead?
- Where will the final project be built?
- Where will the most sales be made?
- Where will your reader resist your idea?
- Where does all of this fit into the strategic direction of the company?
- Where does all this fit into the mind-set of your reader?
- Where is the best place to send this? Home or office?

When?

- When is action required?
- When should the reader receive this?
- When are the deadlines?
- When will the results be seen?

25 ways to connect with your reader

These tips will make your copy more "reader-friendly." We have already touched upon some of these tips in earlier chapters, but I believe they are important enough to quickly revisit. However, the majority of tips in this listing are new and by using them, believe me, you will have a much easier time of "connecting" with your customers.

 **Personalize.**

One of the best ways to get your message across and ensure that it is not full of clichés and "business speak" is to personalize it.

> *For example, an executive who worked for a utility once stood up and said, "My company is a caring company. We want to serve our customers. Our company has a long tradition of service..."*

Stringing a list of clichés together doesn't tell you much, does it?

> *Then another executive stood up and said, "Not long ago, we had to cut the power to a neighborhood because we were repairing some cable. A lady dressed in a bathrobe, her hair sopping wet, came out of a house and yelled for me to come over. Turns out she was in the shower and just got out and was rushing to make a plane in one hour. But her hair dryer didn't work. So I went over, got our portable generator, hooked her hair dryer to it, and she stood in the front yard drying her hair."*

In less than 30 seconds, that story established a picture in the audience's minds, emphasized how deeply the company believed in service and avoided "business speak."

 Be specific.

It's especially important to be specific when you are selling something. I have enclosed two letters here, both selling the same product. Notice how the second, with specific details, is much stronger.

> *Dear Resident:*
>
> *I am writing to tell you about the Blue Star Insurance Company and our great service.*
>
> *Blue Star was founded in 1899 by Thomas Clarke. We have been very popular with our customers, and we have grown dramatically and are now the third largest insurance company on the West Coast. We insure more than 500,000 people, and our assets exceed two billion dollars.*
>
> *Blue Star, as you can expect from a company our size, provides a variety of insurance products, and I know that some of these will meet your needs.*

To find out which product will help you the most, I have enclosed a short form. Please fill it out and send it to me at our home office.

After getting your feedback, I'll contact you with a complete range of recommendations.

Thank you for your attention.

Now notice how this same letter, with specific detail, may even sell a policy.

Dear (insert a personal name):

Are you afraid of a medical emergency hitting your family? Do you worry about a huge hospital bill, costing $100,000 or more, that will bankrupt your family's security?

You're not alone. Many families have the same worry because the average health insurance premium has skyrocketed out of their reach. Instead of paying premiums costing $400 or even $500 a month, they are taking a big chance that tragedy will never strike them.

Good news. I can help. I can offer your family a medical policy that will cost you less than $150 a month. Sound too good to be true? It isn't. This amazing offer is backed by one of the largest and best-financed companies in America. The Blue Star Insurance Company.

Is this policy right for you? Can it save you those sleepless nights of worry? It's easy to find out. Just answer the five questions on the enclosed card and send it back to me. As soon as I get it, I will call you with the best premium for your family.

So fill it out now and let's get together soon. It's time to protect your family and, of course, it's time to get a good night's sleep.

✔ State the benefits loud and clear.

Don't be afraid to boldly list the benefits of your product, your idea, your approach—whatever you're selling (and we're all selling something when we're writing). Don't be shy. Don't make your reader guess at the benefits.

For example, one of the best ads I've ever seen also did the best job I've ever seen of listing benefits. Notice how even the headline promises to save *time, work* and *money*, three things we all want to save. The main headline and the subheads of the ad read as follows. I've left out the ad copy, but it was just as powerful.

Seven ways your Zoysia Grass lawn saves you time, work and money

1. Cuts water bills and mowing by as much as two-thirds
2. Ends reseeding, never needs replacement
3. No need to dig up old grass
4. For slopes, play areas and bare spots
5. Stays green in spite of heat and drought
6. No need to spend money on dangerous chemicals
7. Chokes out weeds and crabgrass all summer

And, of course, this powerful ad had a powerful promise: "Every plug guaranteed to grow in your soil: No *Ifs, Ands or Buts.*"

Also note that the benefits were not just quickly jotted down. Someone obviously did a in-depth study of what people hated most about lawns. They knew the seven key things that bug people most when it comes to growing and taking care of lawns. And because the writers knew their audience so well, they were able to write powerful subheads that not only listed the key benefits but also addressed all the reasons people hate growing grass.

✔ Help your reader understand.

- Whenever possible, put a title on your memo, letter or report that clearly states the problem. Don't write, "The influence on daylight deprivation on children." Do write, "How children suffer when they don't get more than six hours of sunlight." The more specific the title the better. It saves your readers from guessing, and right away, they know what will be presented. They won't need to dig through the whole report seeking the main problem.

- In your first paragraph, state very clearly what you are writing about, what you will cover and your scope for the report.

- Don't present more than one key idea per section. Present the ideas one at a time, support them, explain them, and then move on to the next step or idea.

- Use subheads. They are very effective in identifying what each section is about. Also, readers are turned off by large blocks of text. Subheads break up the text. In addition, subheads let busy executives scan the report and focus on what they deem the most relevant.

- Don't bury numbers and figures in paragraphs. Highlight them with bullets.

- In your conclusion, briefly recap the highlights of your report and the conclusions reached.

✔ Concentrate on the positive.

Don't say, "You won't be sorry to go with Acme Inc."
Do say: "You'll be glad you chose Acme."

Don't say: "I can't see you until after the meeting."
Do say: "I'll see you right after the meeting. Thanks for waiting."

Don't say: "Accidents and poor quality products associated with front-line stress escalate whenever a corporation fails to incorporate stress-reducing activities."
Do say: "Front-line workers dealing with stress will make better products if they have a way to relieve their stress. Some ways may include an on-site gym, counseling sessions...."

✔ Paint a picture.

Paint a picture, *show* the reader what you mean.

Don't say: "Inflation will devastate our economy."

Do say: "Inflation will raise the price of gas by 30 cents, a loaf of bread by 10 cents and a candy bar by a nickel. Perhaps we can afford those small increases, but the average family will have to spend half their income for a house and, instead of buying a new car, settle for used cars."

Another example: A billion dollars is a lot of money. Your readers will understand the concept of that much money better if you paint a picture of how it would affect the average person:

> *A man gave his wife one million dollars, and he told her to go out and spend $1,000 a day. She did. Three years later, she told him the money was gone, and she wanted more. He then gave her $1 billion. He told her to go out and spend $1,000 a day. She didn't come back for 3,000 years.*

☑ Date yourself.

Want a modern image? The University of Chicago says to write the date like this: "1 January 1996." For a traditional image, write "January 1, 1995."

☑ End with power.

Don't end your letter with a cliché, such as "If you need further help, please contact me" or "I'm hoping to speak with you soon." Make your ending say something! State clearly an action you want taken, state clearly when you will call, be aggressive.

☑ The I's don't have it.

Watch how many times you use *I*. Use *you* instead.

Don't say: "I need your help to make this project come together."
Do say: "Your help can make this product sizzle."

Don't say: "I want to tell you about our latest product."
Do say: "Here's some information about our product that can help you cut your budget by 50 percent."

☑ Play with words to spice up your writing.

Every now and then, your reader is delighted to see your sense of humor shine through, pleased to be amused, especially after a day of reading one boring letter after another. So every now and then play with words, like this:

"For 30 years we have watched the classroom change from an arena of learning to one of yearning."

Here's a story showing another way you can play with words:

"I was at a Phoenix Suns game, the first one I ever attended, and I went through the concessions line and ordered a Diet Coke. When I got to the check-out register, the young lady said, "That will be $2." I was sure that price had to be a mistake, so I said, "Two dollars for a Diet Coke—can that be right?" The young lady looked at me and very earnestly said, 'No sir, I don't believe it is right, but that's how much they charge.' "

☑ Use comparisons to give statistics life.

Everyone likes statistics. But statistics, while they may sound impressive, need to be compared to something to give the reader a sense of perspective—an understanding of what the numbers really mean.

"Earned but unclaimed frequent-flier miles offered by airlines total 630 million miles, the equivalent of 90 round trips to the planet Pluto."

"The entire country of Japan—123 million strong—had 25,000 drug-related arrests. New York City had 87,679 drug-related arrests."

☑ Don't just give numbers; paint a picture.

"One dairy cow produces a year's supply of milk for 40 people." (This is much more effective than saying that one cow produces 125 gallons of milk a year.)

"Energy fuels the engine that drives America. In fact, America lives, eats and breathes energy. Americans drive more than 160 million cars, trucks and buses. We watch more than 135 million color television sets. We listen to more than 400 million radios. In fact, every day we Americans consume enough energy to fill a trainload of coal—900 miles long! Every day! If you were waiting at a railroad crossing for this trainload of energy to pass and it was going at 35 miles per hour, it would take more than 24 hours for this train to pass, and then the next day's train would block your path."

"What has 21 square feet of surface area, processes 40 tons of fuel during its useful life, is 95-percent energy efficient, has 80,000 miles of fuel delivery lines, heats and cools itself and has 650 parts named after a small mouse. Give up? It's you."

☑ Always break down big numbers.

Again, for most people who have trouble just balancing their checkbook, big numbers are hard to imagine. Break them down to the smallest unit.

"U.S. residents will spend $13 billion on videos this year. That's about $52 per person."

Each year in the United States, more than 33,000 die from guns. Someone dies from a gunshot every 16 minutes. More Americans were killed by guns in the past two years than during 16 years of fighting in Vietnam. More are killed in a single year than in the past two decades of fighting in Northern Ireland and Beirut combined. The National Rifle Association estimates that there are 200 million firearms in America. A new one comes off the assembly line every nine seconds.

✔ Use numbers to be specific.

You can use facts and figures to illustrate what you are saying.

Don't say: " Americans throw away a lot."

Do say: "Every year, Americans add to their landfills 18 billion disposable diapers, 1.8 billion pens, 247 million tires, two billion razors and blades and 12 billion mail-order catalogs. Enough aluminum is thrown away each year to make 30 jet airplanes."

Don't say: "The updated *Oxford English Dictionary* is big and expensive."

Do say: "The updated *Oxford English Dictionary* has 22,000 pages, fills 20 volumes, weighs 137.72 pounds and costs $2,500."

✔ Use numbers to be funny.

People have a sense of humor. There is nothing wrong with using humorous examples to get your point across. It might even keep your reader awake!

"Americans spend an average of three years of their lives attending business meetings, eight years opening junk mail and two years playing phone tag."

"During the first 13 years of marriage, a happy woman will gain 18.4 pounds and an unhappy one will gain 42.6 pounds. Men gain from 19 to 38 pounds."

✔ Back up your opening statement.

You can't just make a statement like, "When an opportunity arose to help solve two major problems of the decade, Acme jumped in with both feet." You must describe the two problems. Don't make your reader guess.

*"When an opportunity arose to help solve **two major problems** of the decade, Acme jumped in with both feet. The **education problem** is well-known. Our state public schools are graduating a bumper crop of 700,000 functional illiterates every year. That doesn't account for another 750,000 who drop out. The second problem, **voter apathy**, is just as bad. Fifty percent of eligible citizens do not vote in presidential elections..."*

As you can guess, this report went on to show how Acme jumped in to solve the problem.

☑ Talk about the future.

People love to think about the future. So paint a picture of the future to illustrate what will happen if a problem is not solved.

"This is our city in 20 years if we don't take steps now: Our schools are running only one month a year, trash collection is nonexistent and the police force is afraid to go into the streets."

☑ Always explain technical terms to nontechnical readers.

We often use technical terms that are specific to our business when we write. But remember, the outside reader doesn't have the advantage of knowing all these technical terms. So if you use a technical term, explain the term in simple language. For example:

"Let me quickly explain what a kilowatt hour is. You could burn up a kilowatt hour by climbing up and down the stairs of a 100-story building seven times."

☑ Use a name in a crucial spot.

Don't overdo using a person's name in a letter. Experts say use it only once (not including the greeting). When you do use it, use it in a crucial spot: "John, as you'll see by the graph, our sales are dropping drastically."

☑ Use a good analogy to get your point across.

Don't be afraid to put an analogy in your next presentation or speech. Watch an audience: Their heads come up and they pay attention when they are going to hear a good story.

Sometimes getting an abstract concept across is difficult. Instead of wasting a ton of paper and thousands of words, a simple analogy can help. Here's a good example:

> *In preparing for this conference, I couldn't help thinking that modern-day managers could learn something from a football game played here in New York more than 50 years ago.*
>
> *It was 1934. The National Football League championship game. New York Giants against the heavily favored Chicago Bears. Played in bitter cold weather on a field covered with ice. The first half was a comedy of errors, but the Bears managed to bull their way to a 10-3 lead. Bronco Nagurski scored the touchdown.*
>
> *But at half time, the Giants switched from cleats to sneakers— their trainer had gone and borrowed some from the locker room of the Manhattan College basketball team. Suddenly, the Giants had the edge. With their superior traction, they scored four touchdowns in the second half and beat the Bears 30-13.*
>
> *What's the point of my pigskin parable? In the old days, the object of strategic planning was to confront and crush the competition. To bowl them over like Bronco and the Bears did in the first half.*
>
> *Today, it's different. The playing field is often uneven. Conditions can vary widely from one quarter to another. So the object of strategy is to stay one step ahead of the competition. To win by continually adapting. Like the Giants.*

This analogy was used by Monte Haymon, CEO of the Packaging Corporation of America. First, he told his audience a simple story, getting his point across far better than any charts or graphs could. Second, by talking directly to his audience, he built rapport with them. Third, he used plain, simple language. The best CEOs are communicators who know the value of short words. I've mentioned this before, but it's a crucial point.

✔️ Make your letters and memos personal.

Pick a 100-word section out of your letter or memo. Count the personal words: *I, me, we, they,* etc. If it doesn't have 15 personal words, your memo is probably too impersonal and lacks human interest.

✔️ Use handwriting.

Handwriting in the margin of a letter can grab attention, plus it gives the letter a personal touch. The handwritten note may highlight an important item you purposely left out of the letter.

☑ *One* use for passive voice.

Don't blame people.

> *Don't say:* "John caused the computer to crash."
> *Do say:* "The computer went down because of an accident."

☑ Don't focus on features, focus on *benefits*.

> Focus on features: "All our sweatshirts are made of 100 percent cotton."

> *Focus on benefits:* "All our sweatshirts are made of 100 percent cotton, so they don't trap your sweat in. You can run farther because the sweatshirt breathes."

> Focus on features: "Our new heat pump has a 100-SEER rating."

> *Focus on benefits:* "Our new heat pump is so efficient, it can cool your whole house for only five dollars a day. That reduces your utility bill by $50 a month."

> Focus on features: "Walgreens is open 24 hours a day."

> *Focus on benefits*: "We are open 24 hours a day, so when your child wakes up with an 102-degree fever at 3 a.m., we'll have the medicine you need."

☑ Don't flatter.

Avoid sounding like you're trying to flatter too much. For example:

> *Dear Ted:*

> *I was so happy to learn that you had been appointed chairman of the Juvenile Diabetes annual fund-raising auction. You have always been highly dedicated and hard-working, and you certainly deserve this honor.*

> *I understand the magnitude of this auction and want to offer my assistance whenever and wherever you need me.*

> *I know from our many years of working together that you will make this year's auction the most successful we have ever had.*

> *Congratulations once again!*

Let's look at a letter that might sound more sincere to Ted.

Dear Ted:

Wow! Chairman of the Annual Diabetes Auction. It's a tough job, but they picked the right guy for it. Congratulations.

Look, if you need any help, give me a call. I'm sure my public relations background can help you promote the auction, and I'll be glad to write press releases, do PSAs and contact the media for you.

I'll give you a call this Thursday to see if I can help any further. Meanwhile, good luck, and I'll be there to help.

The five key steps of persuasion

1. Don't fool around. State your reason for writing right away.
2. Prove to your readers why the action requested is in their or the company's best interest.
3. Prove why the request makes sense.
4. Give specifics on what actions need to be taken to accomplish your goals.
5. Make the action as easy as possible to take. (For example, "Just give me a call by Friday, and I will take care of it.")

How to turn off a reader

1. Take forever to get to the point. Use prepositions: "In an effort to provide employees with more time for their families, I would like to suggest that we try a four-day work week."
2. In a letter, tell the reader what he or she knows. "You wrote to us on June 4 asking for..."
3. Make the letter more than one page.
4. Use technical terms only you understand.
5. Make your reader guess what the letter is about.
6. Begin your very first sentence with "I." That shows how important you think you are.
7. Use "-ing." A lot. This makes a good, wordy letter. "According to our phone conversation the other day, we are thinking about beginning..."
8. Save important information for the very last paragraph. "Oh, by the way, our sales are plummeting."

How many times have your ears perked up when a speaker says, "Finally," then drones on and on? An old saying among speechwriters is that anyone giving a speech should be made to stand on one leg, then when that leg gets tired, he or she should sit down.

The point is, no matter what you write, know when to sit down. Stop writing when you get to the end. A movie ends when the girl gets her man, an instructional memo ends when your opinion and suggestions have been expressed.

Stop! It's a good word. Know how to apply it to your writing.

Chapter 4 summary

When all is said and done, good writing means good thinking. Writing reflects your thought process on paper. Through that piece of paper, you are trying to show another human being what you are thinking and why it is important. You are selling an idea or concept. Above all, that's why psychology is so important in writing. You are dealing with other people and you must know the best way to approach them, the best way to sell your ideas, the best way to tap into what they want. Simply putting words on a piece of paper won't accomplish these goals. But putting on paper words with a lot of thought behind them will. Never forget that you are writing to another person and never forget to consider the psychological tone or approach you must use.

5

Write for yourself

When I tell people that a key part of business writing is writing for yourself, they are, at first, mystified. Too many people assume that business writing means writing reports, letters or memos to be presented to other people, other readers.

Yet, writing for *yourself* can help you the most. There are two reasons for this. The first is very basic. You only improve at writing by writing. Practicing writing is a lot like hitting a baseball. If you just talk about hitting a baseball then never go out and do it, chances are you will strike out every time. You need to go out and hit, hit and hit some more.

The same is true with writing. If you write only when you have to—for instance, when a report is due—that small amount of writing does little to improve your communication or writing skills. Can you imagine a football team that never practices but shows up for the games? The games would be wipe-outs. The truth is that for every hour of game time, football teams need hundreds of hours of practice.

The same applies to writing. Are you writing just during "game time," or are you putting in the practice hours that will make you shine during "game time"?

The second reason for writing for yourself is simply this: It helps you examine the way you conduct business and the way you approach clients, your bosses, your meetings and other situations. If you write down why you think you made a successful sale, why the boss kicked you out of his or her office, or why the meeting got nowhere, you are developing two skills: writing skills and analytical skills. You will be better prepared to handle a situation when it happens again.

Having said all of that, I ask you: How do you get started on a self-writing program in which what you write is not intended for other readers, but intended to improve your writing, business and interpersonal skills?

Following is an extensive list of exercises. Commit to taking one exercise a week and writing at least a page about it. Developing this habit will help you get in those hours of practice needed to shine during game time. It will give you the valuable practice of organizing your thoughts and putting them on paper, so the next time someone asks you to write something, you won't panic. After all, the more practice you get, the better you get and the more you build your confidence.

So pick a question, in any order you want, and start your once-a-week practice.

Questions for writing to yourself

1. When was the last time you felt insecure in a meeting? What prompted that insecurity, and how can you feel more confident next time?

2. Read a business magazine article or business book whose author's style you like. Copy down 10 lines of his or her style. Then use that style to write 10 lines of your own.

3. Describe your cubicle or office including as many details as possible. Explain why you have certain items in your office and what they represent.

4. Write about the word "angry." When was the last time you were angry in a business setting?

5. Brainstorm a list of new products for your company.

6. Describe the last restaurant at which you ate lunch.

7. Explain what being overworked means.

8. List three different styles of bosses. Combine the best attributes of the three, and describe yourself as the ideal boss.

9. Write an autobiographical page describing the last month in your business life.

10. Compare yesterday to today. Think of how you spent your time both days. Which day was more productive?

11. You bought a new VCR. It ate the first tape you placed in it. Now you are the angry customer. Write a letter of complaint. Then write a paragraph describing how you would respond to that letter.

12. Describe the sounds people make in meetings. Describe the doodles people make in meetings. Describe how they fidget. What do these habits tell you about those people?

13. Open a dictionary and pick a word you don't know. Copy the word and the definition. Look at it, and then throw it away. Now describe what the word means in your own words.

14. Do you remember the first time you met a particular client? Write about your impressions and how your impressions have changed, if they have, over time.

15. Explain why you do or don't drink coffee in the morning. For this exercise write for at least a page.

16. Explain how to find your way to the grocery store closest to your office.

17. Describe the ideal business lunch.

18. Write about the worst business day you've ever had.

19. Describe your best outside vendor and what makes him or her so good.

20. How are a memo and a letter different? How are they alike?

21. Create a list of "office events" that could be in the annual office Olympics.

22. What is the most unethical thing you have done in your business life? What is the most ethical?

23. Describe how you would feel if you had to move to a new office. How should your new office be different from your present one?

24. Imagine you were locked in your office for 24 hours with no chance of escape. What would you do?

25. Write a note to sneak into your boss's pocket.

26. Describe the 10 office habits you really hate.

27. List 20 ways you can use a paper clip.

28. Explain how to operate the copier.

29. Say your boss comes by your cubicle and tosses you a note. It lands on your desk. He or she has discovered your biggest mistake. What is it?

30. Brainstorm types of secretaries. Describe the perfect secretary.

31. Write about the word "ambition."

32. Think about the job in your company you really want. Write a page describing what you need to do to get that job.

33. Describe where you would rather be at this moment and why.

34. Imagine you are in a wheelchair. How does your life change?

35. Describe the best salesperson you know. Why is he or she the best?

36. Explain the logic behind the organization of your office. How could you better organize it?

37. Write a complimentary note to a fellow worker.

38. Imagine you must change careers. Describe your new career and why you chose it.

39. Remember the last time you were really worried at work? Write about that time.

40. How would you feel if you were laid off tomorrow? What would you do?

41. What does "company culture" mean?

42. Say you can attend any conference you want to this year. What conference and what location would you choose?

43. Explain how you would treat a fellow worker who just got chewed out.

44. How do you feel in the morning when it's time to go to work?

45. Describe the funniest business incident you can imagine.

46. Explain to a client what your business does, in 25 words or less. Good luck.

47. List the top 10 people you admire (living or dead) and why.

48. What is the latest office gossip? How does it make you feel?

49. Design your new business card. What does that card say about you?

50. If you left today, who in your office wouldn't you miss? Who would you miss? Why?

51. Write about the word "meeting."

52. Redesign something on your desk. Write it up for submission to an investor.

53. Describe the 10 worst things you can do to not listen during a phone conversation.

54. Describe the top 10 memos you would like to see. Then describe the 10 worst.

55. Write a letter to your old boss. Tell him or her how you have changed.

56. Describe your favorite product and why it is your favorite.

57. Describe the worse communication mix-up you've seen and why it happened.

58. What information do new employees really need to work for your company?

59. Describe whether you feel secure or insecure in your job and why.

60. Draw an organizational chart depicting how you would run the company.

61. You are a mentor to a young employee. What top 10 tips would you give him or her?

62. Write a letter to a teacher or coach you had in college. Tell that person how he or she helped or hindered you.

63. Imagine you're in the most important meeting of your life and realize you have no business cards and no paper or pen to take notes. What does this say about you, and what can you quickly do?

64. You are the office social director. Plan 10 activities the group can do together after work.

65. What are your favorite and least favorite business outfits? Why?

66. When was the last time your office celebrated anything? Describe the celebration and how it reflected the character of your office.

67. Write five things you want people to notice about you.

68. Write five things you don't want people to notice about you.

69. Describe your favorite thinking spot.

70. Where will you be in five years? What must you do to get there?

71. Describe the last meeting you attended.

72. Say you must put out a daily newspaper. But the computers are down. How would you still put out a paper?

73. Describe the 10 excuses you hate.

74. Create a list of requirements for a Top Worker Award.

75. Write clear, concise directions on how to tie a shoe. (It's harder than you think.).

76. Write a letter to a politician explaining what rules and regulations you would like to see to make a better business climate.

77. You are a safety inspector. Walk around your office and write a list of ten hazards you see.

78. What's the best moment you've had with a fellow worker?

79. Explain how the work load is divided in your office. How would you restructure it?

80. Describe 10 reasons a customer should do business with you instead of a competitor.

81. Write about the word "annoy."

82. What part of his or her job does your boss like the least? How do you know that?

83. What are the strengths and weaknesses of your co-workers?

84. Explain your side of a recent argument. Now explain the other person's side.

85. You walk into your office. On your desk is a sealed envelope marked "Confidential." What is in it that will change your career?

86. Write about the word "phony."

87. Write about a new market your company should explore.

88. Explain your worst fears about giving a presentation.

89. Do you like to leave work early or late? Why?

90. Imagine that you are a fly on the wall at a meeting. Describe what you see/experience.

91. Explain the word "confused."

92. What is the most creative business idea you have ever had?

93. What is the best advertising medium to showcase your company?

94. How do you feel when a co-worker is unprepared for a meeting?

95. Write an encouraging letter to a fellow employee. Or write one to yourself.

96. Make a chart of how you spend your time during one day.

97. Imagine your company lost one third of its employees. What work would you eliminate, and what work would you concentrate on?

98. Your favorite fountain pen has been missing for a week. You find it in a co-worker's desk. What do you do?

99. What is your most dominant personality trait?

100. Describe 10 things that make you smile during the work day.

101. Write a note to a friend that has been laid off.

102. You must give up all your job responsibilities except two. Which ones would you keep?

103. List 10 key ways you can make more time for yourself.

104. List and define the 10 most frightening business words you know.

105. Compare the work habits of you and your boss.

106. Write an office "fight song."

107. Write about the word "excel."

108. What does having self-control mean?

109. Who is the brightest person you know and why is he or she so bright or why do you think so?

I close this chapter with E.B. White's advice on writing. All you have to do to be a good writer, according to White, is:

- Place yourself in the background.
- Write in a way that comes naturally.
- Work from a subtle design.
- Write with nouns and verbs.
- Do not overwrite.
- Do not overstate.
- Avoid the use of qualifiers.
- Do not affect a breezy style.
- Use orthodox spelling.
- Do not explain too much.
- Avoid fancy words.
- Do not take shortcuts at the cost of clarity.
- Prefer the standard to the offbeat.
- Make sure the reader knows who is speaking.
- Do not use dialect.
- Revise and rewrite.

Whew! Is that all you need to do? Learning to write well takes a lot of work. And a lot of practice. I can't do the work for you, but I can provide the practice questions. Now, good luck!

Chapter 5 summary

As we close this chapter, please remember that we have done more than give you a list of provocative questions. These questions are designed to make you a better writer, and that can only be achieved by your writing as much as you can. These questions should aid you in the effort. Many people who attend my writing seminars improve their writing skills by teaming up with other people. They may be co-workers, neighbors or friends. Every week, each member of the group chooses a question, then reads what he or she has written to the group the following week. If such a group will help you improve your writing skills, don't be afraid to ask your co-workers or friends to join. The Toastmasters Club meets every week to improve members' speaking skills. A writing club will do the same for your writing skills.

So enjoy the questions, but remember that they are designed to make you a better writer and that can only be accomplished through practice.

6

Press releases

> *"Public sentiment is everything....With public sentiment nothing can fail. Without it, nothing can succeed. He who molds public sentiment goes deeper than he who executes statutes or pronounces decisions. He makes statutes or decisions possible or impossible to execute."*
>
> —Abraham Lincoln

Some of the best writers today work for newspapers. And they can teach you a lot about writing. Their job is to get to the point quickly, give you as much information as possible in a very short space and keep the information interesting enough so that you want to read on. When you think about it, those very same requirements apply to business writing. In this section we'll discuss the techniques for putting together a good press release. Again, you'll note that many of these techniques, ranging from writing strong leads to using an inverted pyramid model, will help make all areas of your business writing stronger.

Know your audience

A press release is a one- or two-page statement sent by companies or organizations to newspapers and TV stations, as well as other media to report something new about the company. It might be an announcement about a new product, a new manager or a new construction project.

Now you may never write a press release in your life, but this chapter is still important to read. Why? First, writing a press release is an excellent exercise in taking the important information and summarizing it. Also, press releases must be the model of clarity, because you are selling an idea. You must be able to capture the reader's attention—or your company will not get the publicity hoped for.

Notice the concepts that make up a press release: clarity, the ability to get to the point quickly and the ability to sell an idea on paper. These skills are the same ones that are crucial to any well-written letter, report or memo! The techniques used in putting together a good press release are the same techniques you can apply to letters, memos and reports.

Any good piece of writing starts with knowing your audience. And sometimes when you write a press release, that isn't easy because every business has numerous audiences.

The press release: key fundamentals

The press release is the most basic and effective way of communicating with the media. For that reason, newsrooms are flooded with hundreds—and in the case of national media, thousands—each week. You must prepare a release that the assignment editor or reporter will not only read, but use to produce the type of story you want. Preparing such a release is a major task. How do you do it? Here are 10 fundamentals you should never forget.

1. **Write only news.** Editors want news. What is news? Ask yourself five questions. Is it: 1) timely, 2) local, 3) unique or unusual, 4) affecting or involving people and 5) provoking human interest? If the answer to any of these is "no," then you probably don't have news. You don't need a news release.

2. **Write in a style and form that will sell itself to that assignment editor or reporter.** He or she usually has time to scan only the first paragraph or two, not the whole release. Thus your format should cover the important information up front. We'll cover this soon in the section on the inverted pyramid.

3. **Make sure you send the release to the right person.** Are the receiving media and reporter correct for your release? For example, don't send a release on a new health product to the fishing editor or a very technical release to a radio station. Send that health release to the medical or science reporter. Send that technical release to the appropriate trade journal.

The news release that talks about a subject with spectacular movement—like a new machine to fight fires—would be ideal for television. The television medium likes stories with visual impact. The effective news release writer knows his or her audience and provides interesting and relevant information.

4. **Write the release in journalistic style.** Journalistic style answers the famous six questions: who, what, when, where, why and how. This is a newspaper story, not an advertisement or a story full of unattributed quotes. The most important information should appear at the beginning of the release with less important or supporting information afterwards. This is the inverted pyramid style. More information on this style later.

5. **Write an effective lead.** The "lead" is the first paragraph. It must boil the story down to as few words as possible. It has to grab the reader. Here's an example: "Construction begins next month on a $90 million office tower in downtown Akron. ABC Real Estate Company says its 48-story building will occupy one city block bounded by First and Second Streets and Main and Apple Avenues." The $90 million and the size of the building, 48 stories, are right up front. Something about numbers, especially *big* numbers, grabs the attention of audiences.

6. **Use an appropriate type of lead.** Leads can range from declarative statements to quotes to teasers. Whatever type you use, make sure it fits the story. For example do *not* write: "How much damage was caused and how many people were injured in a fire earlier today at XYZ Company?" This lead is appropriate for a mystery story. But an editor doesn't have the time to read a mystery. He or she wants the important information now. Use common sense. More information on the types of leads later.

7. **Use short, simple sentences.** Use everyday language. Translate "self-propelled personnel transportation device" to "automobile" or "car." Be sure of your spelling and grammar. (Bad spellers of the world, untie.) Try to use the active voice ("he said," not "it was said"). Avoid adjectives and adverbs. Proofread your release. Double-check names, titles, dates, figures, arithmetic and quotes. Double-check the appropriateness of the release date. Correct typographical errors. Errors leap out at editors and tend to discredit your release.

8. **Mail, fax or hand-deliver your release to the media in enough time for them to use.** Be mindful of editors' deadlines. The sooner you get your release to the media, the better off you are.

9. **Include an appropriate photograph.** Photographs enhance a news release. But make sure the picture will add to it, not detract from it. Don't send an out-of-focus, hard-to-understand picture. Newspapers want a black-and-white glossy at least 8" x 10". Shoot visually exciting pictures. Avoid the "grin-and-grip" photo: people standing against a stark background shaking hands. Often editors use a marginal story because of an interesting or unusual photo.

10. **Include cutlines with your photographs.** A "cutline" is a short paragraph identifying what the paragraph shows. Write it in newspaper style and format. Include your name and telephone number. Paste the cutline onto the back of the photo.

The inverted pyramid

Newspapers have used the inverted pyramid as a story form since the turn of the century. It permits the writer to deliver the most important information in the first few paragraphs. When you use the inverted pyramid, lead off with the most significant information you have. That might be the climax of an event, the theme statement of a speech or the result of an investigation.

Whatever is most significant, the inverted pyramid style demands that you present it, as simply and clearly as possible, in the first paragraph. That first paragraph sets the tone; it advertises the rest of the story.

Your first paragraph, the lead, leads off the story, and in the inverted pyramid style, all else that follows is arranged in descending order of importance. These paragraphs explain or provide evidence to support your lead. And each paragraph contains one idea.

Newspapers adopted this formula for two important reasons. First, the reader may stop reading at any time. So he or she had better get the most important news first. You are not writing a mystery. Get the main point up front. Don't bury it halfway down the column.

Remember, when you are trying to get your point across, you may be writing to an audience distracted by a television or radio blaring in the background. On the average, readers spend only 15 to 20 minutes with a newspaper. Most readers read only a few paragraphs of a story.

The importance of getting your point across is perhaps best illustrated by this story. When the big Johnstown flood hit Johnstown, Pennsylvania, the reporter wired this lead back to his editor:

> *Tonight, God sits on a hill overlooking the flood-ravaged town of Johnstown....*

His editor wired back:

> *Forget Johnstown. Get an interview with God!*

The second reason newspapers use the inverted pyramid style is this: Newspapers want to run as many stories as possible in a limited amount of space. Therefore cutting down your story, without destroying it, is easier if information is presented in descending order of importance.

Following are stories written in an inverted pyramid style. The examples I have quoted appeared in the *Arizona Republic*. By reading your local newspaper, you'll find many such examples. It's a good exercise to go through the articles you like and highlight the way the reporter put the information together. It will help not only your writing skills, but will provide a valuable lesson in organizing important points and presenting them.

The anatomy of an inverted pyramid story

Senate Rejects Gramm's Tax Cut plan
(Note how the headline summarizes the story.)

Washington—Deeply divided Senate Republicans *(who)* could still unite behind a tax cut package *(what)*, but not on the scale proposed by presidential candidate Sen. Phil Gramm *(attribution)*, GOP senators say.

The five-year, $160 billion budget offered by the Texas Republicans was defeated 69 to 31, with 23 of 54 Republicans joining all 46 Democrats in opposition. *(Why: Note this paragraph backs the first one up by offering specific details.)*

(Why is this important?) It was a watershed vote leading up to the expected adoption today of a Senate budget plan that over seven years culls nearly $1 trillion in savings from Medicare, Medicaid and hundreds of programs to eliminate annual deficits.

(Reaction) Gramm had modeled his tax proposal after a slightly larger house plan adopted in April. Its rejection, he said, was "a major setback" for the tax provision in House Republicans' Contract with America.

Violence on TV News Hurts Kids

Television news accounts of a disturbing crime or disaster involving children often traumatize the children who watch them, even if they live hundreds of miles away and have no connection with the event *(what)*.

That is the conclusion of a new study, one of the first in the United States to examine the impact of media coverage on ordinary suburban kids watching the TV news *(attribution)*.

(Why is this study significant?) Most previous studies have focused on the link between the fictionalized violence of television entertainment and increased aggression in children who watch these shows.

(More specific details. Exactly what did the study test?) The latest study examined the impact of the media's coverage of the 1993 kidnapping and murder of 12-year-old Polly Klaas of Petaluma, Calif., an event that grabbed the national spotlight for several months.

(Results) About 80 percent of the 959 children queried for the study two months ago either couldn't stop thinking or dreaming about the crime or were trying desperately to avoid thinking about it, the study indicated.

(Why is this important?) "This rocks our perception of trauma," said Dr. Sara Stein, a psychiatrist at Stanford University who presented the findings at a recent American Psychiatric conference.

(What should we do?) "Kids can be affected by being exposed to the news of a traumatic event, not just by being directly involved. I think this study reinforces the need for very close parental monitoring of what kids watch on the news, and it also calls for better self-regulation by the media."

101 Jobs Lost; Recession Fears Grow

Washington—In ominous economic developments, the nation last month suffered its biggest job loss in four years, and the government's chief forecasting gauge fell a third straight time*(what)*. *(Why is this is important?)* Economists said chances of a recession are growing.

The Labor Department's report *(attribution)* Friday *(when)* on unemployment showed that 101,000 jobs were lost in May, the biggest setback since the nation was pulled out of the last recession in April 1991 *(details supporting first graph)*.

The layoffs were centered in manufacturing and construction *(where)* and caught analysts off guard *(what)*. They had been forecasting an increase in payroll employment of around 175,000 jobs following a loss of 7,000 jobs in April *(why)*.

The so-what? factor

As you write your story in inverted pyramid style, don't forget the "so-what?" factor. Why is this story important? What are the ramifications of this story? The so-what? factor is often addressed in the fourth or fifth paragraph. Note the so-what? paragraphs in bold in the next two examples:

Again, the so-what? question is something your readers is always asking. Remember to tell your readers why the information is important. The examples below, taken from the Associated Press, have the so-what? factor highlighted in bold type.

Hanoi, Vietnam—Eager to meet U.S. conditions for diplomatic recognition, Vietnam turned over about 100 pages of information Wednesday on American servicemen killed or captured during the war.

Vice Foreign Minister LeMai gave the documents to visiting U.S. Rep. Bill Richardson, saying that the data had just been collected from seven northern provinces and that more was expected.

Richardson said the documents included "case-by-case listings of people and what happened...maps, dates and descriptions."

Vietnam wants diplomatic relations with its former enemy so it can attract U.S. investment and technology and discourage Chinese expansionism. Washington has said it will concur only when Vietnam does all it can to clear MIA cases.

The information could strengthen the position of those who support normalizing relations with Vietnam. Backers want President Clinton to act this summer, before the 1996 presidential election campaign gets under way.

Santiago, Chile—In one of the biggest tests of Chile's five-year-old democracy, the government said Wednesday it was willing to use force to jail a former general convicted of ordering a diplomat's slaying in Washington.

Interior Minister Carlos Figueroa said the government will imprison Gen. Manuel Conteras "even if that means using force." Conteras, whose seven-year prison term was upheld by the Supreme Court on Tuesday, vowed not to surrender and claimed he had the support of several army generals.

He did not claim the army was supporting him.

"I talk to my comrades, not to the army," Conteras told reporters at his ranch in southern Chile.

The case marks a milestone for the democratic government. No high-ranking member of the armed forces who served in the 1973-90 regime of Gen. Augusto Pinochet has served prison time for human-rights abuses.

How to write a lead

William Caldwell, a Pulitzer Prize-winning journalist, remembers the best lead he ever heard.

> *One summer afternoon in 1922, I was on my way home from school and my daily stint of work as editor of the village weekly, unhonored and unpaid. Like my father and two uncles, I was a newspaperman. My little brother came running to meet me at the foot of our street. He was white and crying. A telegram had come to my mother. "Pa drowned this morning in Lake George," he gasped, and I am ashamed to be remembering my inward response to that.*

> *Before I could begin to sense such elements as sorrow, despair, horror, loneliness, anger—before all the desolation of an abandoned kid would well up in me, I found myself observing that the sentence my brother had just uttered was the perfect lead. Noun, verb, predicate, period, and who-what-when-where to boot.*

To write a lead that concisely packages the main elements of the story, while compelling the reader to read on, you must know what goes into a lead. The lead should answer six basic questions.

1. Who?
2. What?
3. When?
4. Where?
5. Why?
6. How?

The information for any story you write can be reduced to answer these six questions. For example, let's say you receive this call from the police station.

Man shot in home at 1400 N. Vernon.

Start asking yourself these questions to write your story.

- Who is this man?
- What is his occupation?
- Who shot him?
- When was he shot?
- When was it reported?
- Who reported it?
- How was it reported?

- How long did it take 911 to respond?
- How long did it take to get the man to the hospital?
- How serious was the wound?
- Where was he shot?
- Who else was in the house?
- How many gunshot wounds have occurred this year?
- How does that compare to previous years?
- What are the suspicious circumstances?
- Why was he shot?
- What type of gun was used?
- How old is the man?

You can ask other questions, but every question will fall under one of the categories: *Who, What, When, Where, Why,* or *How.*

You get back to your desk and you start looking over your notes.

- Who? Tom Adams, a student, 14.
- What? He was shot in the side of the head.
- Where? In his bedroom.
- When? The police estimate he was shot at 3:30 p.m.
- Why? Tom was carelessly playing with his father's gun, a Luger.
- How? He thought the chamber was empty .

But as you ask other questions, you learn that Tom's friend had called 911 right away. It had taken 911 one hour to respond because the call was misdirected to a paramedic unit 10 miles from Tom's house. This has happened five times in the past three months. Tom will be okay; the bullet only grazed his scalp, but he was unconscious because of blood loss and the late arrival of the paramedics.

You start writing your lead.

> *A bullet to the head couldn't kill Tom Adams, but the paramedics almost did.*

Cute lead, but no facts.

> *A bullet to the head of young Tom Adams couldn't kill him, but the late arrival of paramedics almost did.*

But wait, when did this happen? How old is Tom? What do you mean by young?

> *On Tuesday afternoon, a bullet to the head of 14-year-old Tom Adams couldn't kill him, but the late arrival of paramedics almost did.*

Okay, you're getting closer. But how late were the paramedics?

On Tuesday afternoon, a bullet to the head of 14-year-old Tom Adams couldn't kill him, but the arrival of paramedics an hour late almost did.

Where did this all happen?

On Tuesday afternoon in suburban Lake Forest, a bullet to the head of 14-year-old Tom Adams couldn't kill him, but the arrival of paramedics an hour late almost did.

But now you're getting to the point at which you have included too much. Is the fact that Tom lived in Lake Forest crucial to the beginning of the story? Probably not; you can insert that later. You might also move Tuesday afternoon down since it would fit more conveniently into a second paragraph that might read...

It all started Tuesday afternoon, when Tom went home to 1400 N. Vernon and began to inspect his father's Luger.

The point is, you need to get as many facts up front. Yet you also have to make an editorial decision. What is crucial to the story? What do you include first, and what do you hold until the second paragraph?

Other types of leads

Thankfully, all leads need not be similar. As in the example of the story of Tom, you determine what type of lead to use. If it is a serious news story, yes, use the "hard" lead: Get to the facts as soon as possible. But with softer stories, you can vary your leads.

Let's look at examples of various types of leads.

The summary lead

This lead is taken from an Associated Press story:

Scientists have identified a powerful appetite suppressant in the brain, a substance that in rats causes them to eat as much as 95 percent less by making them feel full.

"It may be the most potent natural appetite suppressant yet found in rats," said Stephen Bloom of London's Royal Postgraduate Medical School.

Note that the attribution came in the second paragraph. The lead summarized the entire incident.

The description lead

The description lead sets the mood. It gives a feeling, right away, for a person or place. Notice how the two leads following do exactly that. The first is from the *Chicago Tribune*, the second is from *The New York Times*.

> *On January first of last year, a young man named Louis woke around noon. He had the kind of hangover that makes you glance in the mirror just to make sure part of your skull is not actually missing, and a distinct memory of having tried to do some kind of native dance, possibly a Highland fling, the night before.*

> Sarajevo, Bosnia-Herzegovina—*In the winter mists of this battered country, there is a silence deeper than the mere absence of gunfire. People seem muted, hushed as war recedes and anguished retrospection meets fragile hope.*

Note how this lead sets up the personality of the subject right away.

The story lead

This story lead was taken from *The Wall Street Journal*. Notice how the dramatic story gets you involved.

> *Lost in darkness over the mountains of Columbia, the pilots of American Airlines Flight 965 were trying to steer toward the airport Cali. Then came the chilling, synthetic voice from the automatic ground proximity warning system. "Terrain, terrain...pull up, pull up."*

> *The pilots shoved the throttles forward and pulled the nose up sharply. For agonizing seconds, the Boeing 757 tried to climb, almost clearing a mountain ridge. But striking trees near the top of the ridge, the plane lost speed and lift. It smashed into the ground, slid over the top of the ridge and broke into pieces, killing 150 people. Only four survived.*

The contrasting words lead

The following appeared in the *Mesa Tribune*. Note how the words in italics set up contrasting ideas.

> At the *height of* the Valley's recent construction boom, Arizona's second-largest home builder was *sinking into* a sea of red ink. While other companies *prospered*, Tempe-based UDC Homes Inc. *struggled*, weighed down with debt and high-yielding stocks.

> Two weeks ago, UDC toppled into bankruptcy court.

The delayed attribution lead

> *The chairman of a House task force on private property rights said Friday that he has "bent over backward" to ensure a hearing in Phoenix next week will include testimony from all sides of the issue.*
>
> *Rep. John Shadegg, R-Ariz....*

Note that the man's position is more powerful than his name. Plus, people know about task forces; they don't know Shadegg. And his position is more relevant to the story than his name. For these reasons, you would establish his position first, then drop his name down to the second paragraph. That's exactly what the *Arizona Republic* did with the above story.

The stark contrast lead

Notice how this lead, taken from the *Mesa Tribune*, puts two sharply contrasting ideas right next to each other.

> *Stephen Mosher is a friendly man, quick with a joke and good with his nieces and nephews, his family and neighbors said Thursday. But police believe the 34-year-old man also is a rapist who told a friend he attacked women in the East Valley, including...*

The focus lead

The focus lead concentrates on the experience of one person, then expands the focus to cover a broader issue. It is a good technique because right away it shows the human side of major news stories. It draws readers in, and, like the examples below show, the Associated Press uses it in many of their stories.

> Tuzla, Bosnia-Herzegovina—*After operating for fifteen hours on scores of wounded, surgeon Zlatko Berberovic rushed home Friday, grabbed a sandwich and a shower, then rushed back to operate on dozens more.*
>
> *His city, so far mostly spared the carnage that has ravaged Bosnia, was staggering from the deadliest shelling of Bosnia's more-than-three-year-old war....*

> Dover, England—*Sitting aboard the ferry Pride of Burgundy as it steamed toward France, Kenneth Poulter said he had no intention of trying the Channel Tunnel, the 31-mile undersea link that was supposed to revolutionize travel between Britain and the continent.*

*"I can't see the point of sitting down there in a long tunnel,"
Poulter said, heading for a three-day weekend in France. "We
regard the actual crossing as part of the vacation, and the ferry is a
much more pleasant way of doing that."*

*At more than $15 billion, the tunnel is one of the most expensive
building projects in history....*

*Burbank, California—Martha Sias had no idea what she was
producing before she was laid off from her high-security job as an
assembler of military aircraft parts for the Lockheed Corp., but she
says she was "very good at it."*

*"You have your blueprints here; you have your parts here," she
said. "You sit in a little cubicle and you're making that one part.
What it goes to, where it goes to, they don't tell you."*

*Like so many of the hundreds of thousands of jobs making
military and aerospace equipment that were the underpinnings of
the California economy for decades, it was great work. "You've got
good benefits, good money, and you're always moving up," Sias
said. "Your money never stays the same. It's always increasing."*

*But in November 1993, Sias' dream job ended. At 43, she was
caught in a tidal wave of layoffs caused by declines in military
spending....*

The statistics lead

*Over the past decade, the cost of replacing a stolen or wrecked
automobile has risen 90 percent; the cost of auto parts has risen 56
percent; the cost of labor for auto repairs has risen 75 percent;
doctor's fees have risen 108 percent; and hospital room costs have
gone up 151 percent.*

And Republicans claim inflation is dead...

The one-clever-sentence lead

The "fried-chicken" lead, written by Edna Buchanan, illustrates the
classic one-clever-sentence lead. Calvin Trillin tells the "fried-chicken"
story this way.

*The fried-chicken story was about a rowdy ex-con named Gary
Robinson, who late one Sunday night lurched drunkenly into a
Church's outlet, shoved his way to the front of the line, and ordered
a three-piece box of fried chicken. Persuaded to wait his turn, he*

reached the counter again five or ten minutes later, only to be told that Church's had run out of fried chicken. The young woman at the counter suggested that he might like chicken nuggets instead. Robinson responded by slugging her in the head. That set off a chain of events that ended with Robinson's being shot dead by a security guard. Edna Buchanan covered the murder for the Herald—there are policemen in Miami who say it wouldn't be a murder without her—and her story began with what many still regard as the classic lead: "Gary Robinson died hungry."

The provocative question lead

Often, just asking your reader a provocative question is all you need to hook his or her attention. This one-line question from *The Wall Street Journal* proves that point:

Are your wages set in China?

The delayed revelation lead

Sometimes, it's okay to tease your readers along, to entice them into the story. This lead from *The New York Times* does exactly that.

He rented movies, playing one about a Colorado football team over and over. He wore a favorite T-shirt with a quotation from Thomas Jefferson. He once changed cheap motels so he could watch the X-rated spice channel. He always washed the dishes.

These surprisingly ordinary activities are little pieces of the puzzle that is the greatest remaining mystery of the case charging Timothy J. McVeigh with blowing up the Federal Building in Oklahoma City, killing 168 people. Why would he do it?

Chapter 6 summary

This chapter has been about much more than writing press releases and leads for newspaper stories. The same techniques that reporters use can also be used by you to make your reports, memos and letters more interesting and more informative.

The broader lesson contained in this chapter is this: There are excellent examples of writing (and bad examples, also) everywhere you turn. Even your daily newspaper has writing tricks that will make you a better writer. But to discover these techniques, you need to go through a story you like and carefully analyze it, much as we did with the examples in this chapter.

If you want to become a better writer, stick with it. And remember the advice of science fiction author, Ray Bradbury, about what it takes to be a good writer:

> *"Success is a continuing process. Failure is a stoppage. The man who keeps moving and working does not fail....If you write a hundred short stories and they're all bad, that doesn't mean you've failed. You fail only if you stop writing. I've written about 2,000 short stories; I've only published about 300 and I feel I'm still learning. Any man who keeps working is not a failure...."*

Appendix 1

Warm-up exercises

The following exercises are intended to get your "writing muscles" limbered up. If you're just sitting there looking at a blank piece of paper, these exercises, much like jumping jacks, will get your blood flowing, making it easier to move onto that letter, memo or report.

Warm-up exercise 1

Sometimes the best way to start writing is to make a list. Let's say your company is moving across the country, and you have to send a letter to employees telling them the main things they need to know about moving. That could cover a lot of ground. So you don't get nervous and forget anything, simply start a list of words you associate with moving:

• Boxes	• Cost	• Timing
• Stress	• Packing	• Storage
• Mail	• Fragile	• Address
• Phone	• Movers	• Cleaning

Well, you get the idea. Now simply add your own ideas to this list, and then write a one-page letter to employees reminding them of the important things they must not forget when they move.

Warm-up exercise 2

Hey, you're an inventor. Congratulations! But no one has any idea what you have invented, what it is good for or how it can help all of us.

Your task is to make up an invention. That's right. Right now. Then imagine you are sitting in front of a banker who will give you lots and lots of money to produce this great invention. But she's too busy to talk to you. She says, "Go home, put it in writing, bring it back and I'll present your idea to the loan committee."

Good luck. The future of the world—well, at least the future of your invention—is resting on how well you can sell the idea and the need for it to the loan committee. But wait...

The invention should, of course, have a snappy name!

Oh yes. Before you start writing about your invention, having a picture of it in front of you could help, so draw your invention below.

Invention name: _____

Okay, so you're a writer, not an artist!

Now convince the bankers to give you lots of money to finance your idea.

_____

_____

_____

_____

_____

_____

_____

_____

_____

_____

_____

_____

_____

_____

_____

_____

_____

_____

_____

_____

_____

_____

_____

_____

_____

_____

_____

_____

_____

_____

Warm-up exercise 3

It's your turn to play movie critic. Think about a video or recent movie you liked or hated. Now write a review of it for the paper. Remember, you are trying to convince people that this movie is good or bad or so-so. Tell them why you liked it and why you didn't like it. And as you would with any good review (or business report), include positive suggestions for how the movie could have been changed. Let your audience know as much about the movie as possible *in 500 words or less* (about one typed page, single-spaced).

Warm-up exercise 4

When you think about it, a newspaper editorial is a lot like a good business report or letter. The writer tells you what he or she is for or against, gives concrete examples to demonstrate why and then offers a solution to whatever the problem is.

Write an 800-word editorial about something you want changed. Explain what you want changed, why you want the change, what the change will accomplish and how it should be implemented.

Warm-up exercise 5

You have a lot of great ideas, but your boss wants you to cover your best one in two pages. How can you do this? One of the best warm-up exercises to help you is to write a radio commercial about your idea. In your commercial, you can persuade the boss to move to new offices, to buy a new product or to lay off employees (how depressing!). The point is *to sell* the boss on an idea. Any idea.

Have fun with it first. Write your radio commercial on the main points of your idea and why your boss should go for it. The radio commercial can be only one minute long. Write it, and then read it out loud while a friend times you.

If you can put your idea into a one-minute radio spot, you won't have any trouble covering it in two pages.

So give it a try.

Warm-up exercise 6

You have just had a brilliant idea! Instead of building more freeways, more schools or bigger houses that use more energy, the best way to use our existing resources and save our planet is to create small people. You might be six feet tall. Well, your children should grow to only four feet. And their children should be genetically programmed to be only three feet tall.

Why is this a good idea? How will it change the world? Write a two-page letter to your boss—the head of a DNA lab—on why you should proceed with this project.

Appendix 2

Exercises

The previous exercises were designed to be fun, to get your writing blood flowing. The following exercises have a different intent. They are designed to get you *thinking*, to help you hone your skills. You don't need to do them all at once, but if you do one a night or one a week, you'll notice a gradual change for the better in your writing. I have given proposed answers to the exercises. Your solution may be different from mine, but if you feel you've delivered a good, concise, strong piece of writing, that's what matters!

Exercise 1

The memo below went to customer service representatives and front-line employees, many of whom speak in plain, simple English and have no desire to impress their supervisor. Yet the following memo is typical of a person using the wrong tone, the wrong words and the wrong approach to impress an audience. In short, it's written in "corporate speak." Now how would you put this memo in English?

Currently, if an Equalizer customer with a debit account balance requests to be terminated from the plan, the debit amount is considered "due" at the time of termination. If the account balance has not been paid prior to the next billing, it will appear as a "past due" amount, a service disconnect will print on the bill and further collection activity will take place. Often, the length of the time between the termination from the plan and the next billing is only a few days.

We recognize the problems that this short time span for payment has caused many of our customers and are making revisions to the system to lengthen the time frame. The changes will allow the debit amount to display as "Equalizer Account Balance Due" on the next month's bill and will automatically prohibit any collection activity during that month.

_____

_____

_____

_____

_____

_____

_____

_____

_____

_____

_____

_____

_____

_____

_____

_____

_____

(proposed solution on page 186)

Exercise 2

Here is a paragraph taken from a letter. Good luck reading and re-writing it, and may common sense be with you!

Interest in broadening competition in the electric power industry has also increased interest by a number of entities to require that access to our utility transmission lines be mandated by a regulatory agency. At the heart of these proposals is the idea that increased transmission access will promote competition and result in less costly electricity. The economic benefits, however, may not transfer to all customers in a utility's service territory.

_____

_____

_____

_____

_____

_____

_____

_____

_____

_____

_____

_____

_____

_____

_____

_____

_____

_____

_____

_____

_____

_____

_____

_____

_____

(proposed solution on page 186)

Exercise 3

Here are two opening paragraphs from a CEO presentation. In it he is discussing steps the electric utility industry can take to appease environmental groups. The environmental groups want to reduce emissions from power plants that contribute to global warming. Note that the CEO does not even agree that global warming even exists. He downplays the problem by calling it *global climate change*:

> Global Climate Change may be the biggest issue we will be asked to address in our service to our industry. My objective here today is to describe the scope of activities taking place on this issue at the international level and within the United States. These activities are important for us to understand as we probe the dimensions of the issue and what actions our industry takes in response to the many facets of the issue. There are many solutions we can help to implement. These range from international treaties limiting carbon emissions to strict local regulations.
>
> Let me say at the outset that, in my view, in addressing any environmental issue of significant dimension, such as Global Climate Change, we are inevitably faced with risks to our industry. However, I also believe that in any issue such as this, we are also presented with opportunities. I believe that by focusing on this opportunity and developing responses to maximize the gain we can obtain from the issue, we minimize the risks.

(proposed solution on page 186)

Exercise 4

Here is another opening from a speech. By the way, the audience for this speech was a group of high school students. Remember your audience; remember the way they talk. Be creative in your solution.

> My goal today is straightforward: to convince you that the problems of
> population growth and sustainable development are so important and so
> interesting that you will decide to do something about them. I'm talking
> about development as the process of socioeconomic improvements on
> people's lives around the world.

(proposed solution on page 187)

Exercise 5

Here is another memo from the corporate world. Put this one in plain, simple English.

The attached catalog is forwarded to assist you and your personnel to plan your general computer training needs. It is carefully organized to ensure that a sequence of training can be followed which will result in a progressive improvement in computer literacy. We strongly urge that classes not be scheduled unless the student has ongoing access to the necessary computer equipment or software. Experience has shown that long delays between training and productive use of the knowledge gained invariably negates most of the training.

_____
_____
_____
_____
_____
_____
_____
_____
_____
_____
_____
_____
_____
_____
_____
_____
_____
_____
_____
_____
_____

(proposed solution on page 187)

Exercise 6

The following is an excerpt from a report that the Acme company is using to introduce its company culture. Even though seven characteristics are explained, this example show one. Please rewrite this example so the reader will have a better understanding of what you are really saying.

The following seven characteristics, along with their accompanying definitions, have been identified by Acme senior management as critical to the type of company Acme needs to become. These will be, of course, refined, added to, modified and made operational over time. What follows represents the starting point for building the working environment of the "New Acme Corporation."

These characteristics can only become part of the company's culture with considerable effort. Our success in incorporating them into the fabric of Acme depends on several factors, including selecting personnel in light of their ability to function in such a setting, managerial behaviors which demonstrate commitment to these characteristics, and management systems (budgeting, evaluation, performance management...) which reinforce these characteristics.

1. Customer driven: Actively seeking ways for most effectively employing limited available resources in a manner which provides excellent service to customers in terms of what they value from Acme. This includes being responsive to customer needs and requests, defining how each department can contribute to lowering the price component of our product and excellent service (from the customer's perspective), and behaving as though serving the customer is the only rationale for Acme's existence. Line departments have an obligation to serve the external customer in this spirit. Staff departments must service their internal customers in a manner which supports high value service to external customers. Loyalty is to the customer, not the function.

_____

_____

_____

_____

_____

_____

_____

_____

_____

_____

_____

_____
_____
_____
_____
_____
_____
_____
_____
_____
_____
_____
_____
_____
_____
_____
_____
_____
_____
_____
_____
_____
_____
_____
_____
_____
_____
_____
_____
_____
_____
_____
_____
_____
_____

(proposed solution on page 187)

Exercise 7

This letter was written to a state legislator seeking his support. Yes, it could use a little improvement:

Dear Speaker of the House:

I am writing to express support for HB 2137, which provides for mandatory seat belt use in Arkansas.

The evidence that is now available from other states (and from our own company policy mandating seat belt use in corporate vehicles) clearly shows that the expanded use of seat belts arising out of *mandatory seat belt laws* saves lives and reduces injuries. The benefits from this expanded use of seat belts, in terms of avoidance of human tragedy reflected in accident victims who do not use their belts, is almost incalculable.

The increased cost created by injured, unbelted passengers in increased insurance premiums, lost wages for the employee, lost production time for the company and costs incurred in training new employees to fill the place of an unbelted accident victim is staggering.

Arkansas, the most dangerous state in the nation in which to drive, is the only southern state which has failed to adopt a mandatory seat belt law. Subsequent to the increase in speed limits on rural interstates in Arkansas, there has been a significant increase in deaths (58 percent from April 15 to November 30, 1994). Other statistical evidence indicates there is an injury-related accident occurring in Arkansas every 8.4 minutes.

It is our belief that the people of this state will support a reasonably enforced seat belt law. The benefits to be obtained from such a law by the avoidance of expanding human tragedy and the reduction of costs incurred are obvious.

On behalf of my company and its employees, I urge your support of HB 2137.

Very truly yours,

_____
_____
_____
_____
_____
_____
_____
_____
_____
_____
_____
_____
_____
_____
_____
_____
_____
_____
_____
_____
_____
_____
_____
_____
_____
_____
_____
_____
_____
_____
_____

(proposed solution on page 188)

Exercise 8

Question: What is the key accounts program?

Answer: The Key Accounts Program provides a systematic approach to help us build and maintain positive business relationships with a selected number of our major commercial and industrial customers.

_____

_____

_____

_____

_____

_____

_____

_____

_____

_____

_____

(proposed solution on page 188)

Exercise 9

Steve said if his group administers or develops a marketing program which they know will benefit a certain customer or group of customers, they will work through a Key Account representative in offering that program to the customer.

_____

_____

_____

_____

_____

_____

_____

_____

_____

_____

(proposed solution on page 188)

Exercise 10

This letter is trying to convince you to invest in an energy-efficient home. Yet, all the facts are buried in the copy. Pull out the main facts, figure out what will really sell the reader and then rewrite it.

As a smart and serious home buyer, you want to know *why* you should choose a Total Electric Energy-efficient Home over any other. We're happy to tell you the difference is significant energy savings.

To begin with, when you choose a Total Electric EEH home, you're saving about $1,000 right off the top over what you would pay for a dual-energy home. That's because it costs that much to install the extra equipment for the additional energy source.

Add to this the high-efficiency electric heat pump—the most cost-efficient climate-control system available, offered only in Total Electric Energy-efficient Homes. This all-in-one heating and cooling system can save you up to $150 *year after year*.

Other EEH specifications include ceiling insulation rated R-30 or higher, and high R (resistance) values for wall insulation. These high standards mean more comfort and more than $45 in savings each year.

Effective attic ventilation releases hot air in the summer, preventing "over-heating." But in the winter, when hot air is precious, heat losses through air ducts are virtually eliminated because they are insulated, wrapped and lined.

Weather-stripping on all exterior doors and windows, including the door into the garage, also keeps at least $30 from seeping through the cracks annually.

Your Total Electric EEH homebuilder also designs homes with Arizona's abundance of sunshine in mind. Strategically placed windows bathe living areas in light and provide beautiful views, yet actually take up only a small percentage of wall area, reducing excessive warmth and cooling bills.

Window-shading devices such as sun screens, reflective film, dual panes or awnings save you an additional $80 each year, and save the color and elegance of your draperies and carpeting as well.

It's clear the Total Electric Energy-efficient Home offers energy savings that make a difference.

Call me and I'll tell you more.

_____

_____

_____

_____

_____

_____

(proposed solution on pages 188-189)

Exercise 11

This exercise is interesting because it shows what can happen when you don't break information up into small amounts that your reader can easily digest.

Subject: Employee Savings Plan

I'm pleased to announce that beginning with payroll deductions January 15, the "match" of Acme common stock made by the company on behalf of Employee Savings Plan participants will be applied up to the initial six percent of an employee's pre-tax contribution. The current level of contributions eligible for a match is five percent.

If you are currently contributing a minimum of six percent on a pre-tax basis, the company match will automatically be applied, and thus you will not have to fill out a Change Form. However, if you are currently contributing less than six percent on a pre-tax basis and want to increase your pre-tax contribution in order to take advantage of the more liberal matching policy, please contact Employee Benefits and request a Change Form.

_____
_____
_____
_____
_____
_____
_____
_____
_____
_____
_____
_____
_____
_____
_____
_____
_____
_____
_____
_____

(proposed solution on page 189)

Exercise 12

To: All Employees

Subject: Changes coming to telephone system

Several important changes will be made to the Acme telephone system, beginning in March, that will affect the way many Acme employees make calls inside and outside the company. Growth in calling volume and the need to manage and protect expensive telecommunication resources efficiently are making the changes described below necessary. Communication System anticipates that the greatest impact to users will be relearning dialing habits and understanding the new long-distance calling procedures.

Detailed use instructions will be provided on the new features at the time they are implemented in each area of the company.

This memo is to give our users advanced information on impending changes and allow questions prior to implementation.

Eight-Digit Long-Distance Calling Authorization Code Change

New authorization codes will be eight digits in length, and all long-distance callers will be assigned new codes for security reasons. An authorization code (four digits for Acme, six digits for suppliers) is required to access the long-distance control system (now Infoswitch) and to track responsibility for long-distance charges. (EXAMPLE: an existing Infoswitch number, 888-1234-602-371-7171, will be dialed on the new system as 9-1-602-371-7171—(PROMPT)—12345678, where 12345678 is the new authorization code). Users will be prompted by 10 fast beeps at the proper time to enter the Authorization Code.

The Infoswitch system is obsolete and unmaintainable and will be replaced by A CALL DETAIL RECORDING system that operates in conjunction with call Authorization software in each PBX.

The PBX network attempts to complete long-distance calls via a least-cost routing system process that will utilize Acme's communications transmission facility (microwave, fiber optics, and cable) whenever possible. Most Acme inside-company calls and a substantial number of in-state long-distance calls can be completed in this manner without long-distance costs....

At this point I will spare you more anguish. The memo went on for three more pages. But as you rewrite this memo, remember to concentrate on what your audience needs to know.

(proposed solution on page 189-190)

Exercise 13

Overcoming Skepticism:
Making the Realignment Process Work

No matter how it is carried out, though, the realignment of a company's employees has a traumatic effect on any organization, especially if the realignment involves a substantial staff reduction in a company that has the core cultural values of job security and employee loyalty. Realignment enables management to seize the opportunity provided by such a difficult period to make progress toward strategically directed performance goals and to establish the basis for a new organizational culture.

Realignment is comprised of a handful of essential components, all of which must be carried out in a coordinated way using a system of checks and balances. Piecemeal application defeats both the effectiveness and integrity of the concept. For example, we have seen some organizations implement an internal placement program (designed to help employees locate jobs elsewhere in the organization) with unsatisfactory results because the effort occurred within a strategic vacuum and without senior management oversight.

Effective implementation has the requirement of meticulous attention to detail and effective senior management visibility throughout the realignment and recovery period. Employees are typically suspicious and skeptical of management's ability to successfully complete the process. However, as it unfolds, realignment provides validation of management's seriousness through both the integrity with which the process is followed and the resulting selections and placements that are implemented internally and externally.

The key implementation steps for realignment....

Comment: This article, intended for a professional journal, goes on for another 15 pages, not counting the "required" impressive graphs and charts that look like they were drawn by an engineer.

_____
_____
_____
_____
_____
_____
_____
_____
_____

_____

_____

_____

_____

_____

_____

_____

_____

_____

_____

_____

_____

_____

_____

_____

_____

_____

_____

_____

_____

_____

_____

_____

_____

_____

_____

_____

_____

_____

_____

(proposed solution on page 190)

Exercise 14

Corporate Headquarters' Heating, Ventilating and Air Conditioning

Property Services is requesting your assistance towards the cost-effective operation of the Corporate Headquarters (CHQ) building. In an effort to optimize building operations and minimize costs, Property Services is changing the operation of the heating, ventilating and air conditioning at CHQ.

The Acme Company has redesigned and installed a new heating, ventilating and air conditioning (HVAC) system in the CHQ building. This new control system uses a computer to adjust and control the heating and cooling times and temperatures to minimize the costs associated with operating the HVAC system.

On April 1, Acme will begin operating the HVAC system in the CHQ building to insure design temperatures are maintained during "Standard Operating Hours." Standard Operating Hours are 8 a.m. through 6 p.m. Monday through Saturday. The HVAC system for the general office space will normally be "OFF" during non-standard operating hours.

Should any department/area require office space heating and cooling outside the Standard Operating Hours (such as departments working 7 a.m. to 4 p.m.), arrangements will need to be made with Property Services to override the computerized HVAC control system.

(proposed solution on page 190)

Exercise 15

Safety Bulletin

An accident that happened in May requires the need to put out some information that has been stressed many times before. Namely, watch for others around the truck when operating the stiff legs and make sure their feet are in the clear.

It seems that in a division, a line crew was in the process of putting away a boom and getting the line truck ready to move. Employee #1 was operating the controls, saw Employee #2 standing near the left rear stiff leg. Since Employee #2 was on the left side, Employee #1 raised the stiff legs on the right side of the truck. He then raised the left front stiff leg. When the left front stiff leg came up, weight that had been held up by the left front stiff leg was transferred back to the left side and caused the left rear stiff leg to settle down on Employee #2's right foot, crushing his big toe. When the right side stiff legs were raised, the left rear came up off the ground, allowing Employee #2 to slip his foot under it while he was putting away tools.

Again, we need to remind you: Whenever anyone is operating the stiff legs on a vehicle, it is imperative that the operator look before he or she moves a handle and always make sure anyone near the truck is in the clear of any stiff leg.

Also, it is the responsibility of anyone who is working around a stiff leg to be aware that outriggers may move and to stay away from them.

(proposed solution on page 191)

Exercise 16

Your main effort in this exercise should be on the concentration of eliminating all the unnecessary verbiage that is buried within the informational content. In other words, make it short and to the point.

Jo Lou, president, called public attention Friday to the organization of a demonstration to be held by the Phoenix Neighborhood Alliance. The demonstration is planned as a protest against the city's negligence in demolishing a vacant house in the Phoenix area. Children who live in the area view the house as a playhouse, although it is filled with broken glass and garbage, and rats and other hazards are often reported there. The Phoenix Neighborhood Alliance demands and hopes the city will move quickly to demolish the house and that this demolition will be motivated by the demonstration.

Big hint: This should be reduced to 23 words or less.

_____

_____

_____

_____

_____

_____

_____

_____

That's it. You don't need any more space. Trust me!

(proposed solution on page 191)

Exercise 17

Subject: Attitude Survey Focus Groups

This memo is to request your participation in a focus group to help analyze and interpret data from a portion of the recently completed attitude survey. The group will meet only once for approximately four hours in the Sunset Room on the fifth floor.

We have decided on this course of action because it is clear to us that we don't totally understand the concerns of our employees specifically enough. We also believe that for us to effect the kind of change that needs to occur, we have to be certain that every member of management understands specifically what is expected.

Attached to this memo is a list of items from the attitude survey which received poor ratings. In each category there are statements which generally identify the dissatisfaction. It is our goal to change these generalities into specifics so that we can ensure that all foremen, supervisors, managers and officers have clear and specific examples of behavior which contribute to employee dissatisfaction in order that we may properly and expeditiously deal with the issues.

Your role as a focus group member is to identify specific examples of the general statements in the space provided on the attached summary. Your input on these issues is invaluable and will go a long way toward helping us better understand employees' concerns.

Hint: You are trying to recruit employees for a focus group. Would this letter get you excited and make you want to show up?

_____

_____

_____

_____

_____

_____

_____

_____

_____

_____

_____

_____

_____

_____

(proposed solution on page 191)

Exercise 18

The following was written for a local automobile association magazine. The writer was supposed to give a brief history of his business and tell the association members that he was taking over the business from his father. He did a fairly good job, but notice this piece has no sense of rhythm. Rewrite it so it has a better sense of flow, a better sense of rhythm. Also note the long paragraphs with too many ideas crammed into them. By the way, this is a long letter. Don't feel the need to rewrite all of it. Just pitch a few paragraphs and rewrite them to give you an idea of how they should be changed.

This is the story of the oldest continuously operated used car dealership in the state of Arizona. My father Roman Sarwark started Sarwark Motors in 1942. He had come to Arizona from Indiana after almost dying of tuberculosis. The doctors said he had to move where it was warmer in order to regain his health. He established his business at the corner of 16th St. and Van Buren where it remains today, as Consolidated Auto Sales. When the business was started, Van Buren could be compared to the Bell road of today. The new car dealers were located around Central and Van Buren. Over the years they moved north, but we stayed. For a while in the 50s and 60s, he had tried his hand at new car franchises, one of which was a Volvo dealership. It was also during this time that he tried the mobile home business. During the mid-60s this was a very good business. In 1971 we sold over 300 mobile homes, which was quite an accomplishment. In 1980, he decided that it was best to discontinue the mobile home business and return to what he knew best, the car business.

It was in the early years that he discovered the value of carrying contracts for his customers, or as it has come to be known, the "Buy-Here-Pay-Here" business. He knew that these were good customers; but due to financial conditions, they couldn't get bank financing. I can remember looking at records and seeing deals in which the car sold for $995, with a $60 down payment and $15 weekly payments. Then, as now, most of these people paid for their cars. Through the years, inflation has taken its toll; now most of our cars sell for more than $4,000. We have many customers whose parents bought cars from my father many years ago. They like the casual family atmosphere of our business. A permanent feature at our cashier's window is a jar of candies that are given to anyone who asks. We also have a stock of toys to give to children of our customers.

I started working for my father full time in about 1972, learning the business from the ground up. As the years progressed, I gradually assumed more and more of the duties that my father had been doing in regards to running the business.

(cont.)

Now, at the age of 82, he has decided that it is time I take over as President of Consolidated Auto Sales. He will remain and be active as an advisor but will play less of a role in the day-to-day operation of the company. I realize that I must fill the position that my father has had for so many years. This will be a challenge, but I feel that I am up to it. I must evaluate our strategies in the light of today's business climate. Most of them still work very well, but some must be changed to allow us to continue and thrive for another 50 years. This is a very crucial time in the history of the used car business. Right now the competition is stronger than I have ever seen it. These challenges can be changed into opportunities which will allow us to grow and prosper in the years to come.

_____
_____
_____
_____
_____
_____
_____
_____
_____
_____
_____
_____
_____
_____
_____
_____
_____
_____
_____
_____
_____
_____
_____
_____
_____
_____
_____
_____
_____
_____
_____

(proposed solution on pages 192-193)

Exercise 19

Subject: Affirmative Action/Employee Relations

Over the past few months, there has been a growing concern that the recent reorganization of the Human Resources function caused Acme to dismantle its commitment to affirmative action and equal employment opportunities.

Nothing could be further from the truth. Part of that confusion arose because we did not fully communicate the role of Employee Relations Representatives, which were intended to be a centralized "full service" focal point for all employees' concerns in the event that the supervisor and the employee cannot reach resolution of employment-related problems, including those relating to equal employment opportunities....

(proposed solution on page 193)

Exercise 20

Rewrite the following paragraph to give it at least some sense of rhythm. Notice the dull subject-verb, subject-verb format.

> "Composting/Recycling—What It Takes to Expand Programs" was the theme of a March 1994 West Coast Conference sponsored by the *BioCycle Journal of Composting & Recycling*. More than 300 participants gathered at Holiday Inn on the Bay in San Diego, California, for three days of networking and information-sharing. Speakers represented private businesses and organizations, educational institutions, public agencies and all levels of government. Topics focused on program and facility management, regulatory impacts, scientific research and economic opportunities. Special efforts were made to facilitate group sharing in the Composting Sessions. An Open Forum topic, "Increasing the Role of Composting on the West Coast," provided participants with an opportunity to express their views and to ask questions of a panel of policy makers, legislators and composters.

(proposed solution on page 193)

Exercise 21

The whereabouts of the long-awaited recovery (outside of the single-family housing sector) remains a mystery. Actually a recovery is occurring in some sectors, but in general it is so anemic that it simply doesn't feel good. Housing permits are up significantly, and even retail sales have picked up. That has not translated into meaningful growth in overall wage and salary improvement, however. In fact, a decline in expectations has been occurring for many months now, as can be seen by the long series of downward revisions in both employment and personal income estimates by our panel. It is clear that the historically high levels of debt on the part of consumers, business and government remain a drag on our economy. The present low levels of inflation make debt burdens seem that much higher because the dollars with which they are paid back are more valuable in real terms.

(proposed solution on page 193)

Exercise 22

Hint: The use of bullet points would help this job requirement document.

Duties: The incumbent is fully responsible for the work accomplished by subordinate housekeeping aids working in patient, clinical and administrative areas on the weekend shift. Incumbent schedules, conducts and documents all housekeeping and classroom training to include new employee orientation, procedure and safety training, as well as recurring and refresher training for all housekeeping aids on day, evening, and weekend shifts. Will assume day-to-day supervisory responsibilities for day-shift housekeeping aids when day-shift housekeeping aids and foreman are on leave. Incumbent is delegated full authority for deciding what work will be accomplished, who will do the work and when and how the work will be accomplished, as well as responding to requests to correct problems. Is responsible for approving or disapproving requests for annual or sick leave, determining AWOL charges, and requests for advance leave or leave without pay. Independently conducts and documents verbal counseling, prepares and issues written counseling and admonishments, and formulates written recommendations to superiors for reprimands, suspensions, and removal actions as well as annual written ratings on subordinates' performance and maintains sufficient written documentation to support rating levels given.

(proposed solution on page 194)

Exercise 23

Nearly all participants in the welfare reform debate agree that the welfare system should place a greater emphasis on preparing recipients for work and helping them find jobs. As the Congress and state legislators consider various welfare reform proposals which seek to place a greater emphasis on work, it is important to consider the labor market prospects of mothers who receive AFDC. Many mothers receiving AFDC have very low skills; the majority of them have not graduated from high school and have no previous work experience.

(proposed solution on page 194)

Exercise 24

Change these *negative* thoughts to *positive* thoughts:

1. Negative: Because you failed to say what size shirt you wear, we cannot send it.
   Positive:

2. Negative: We're sorry we cannot offer you television spots for $1,000.
   Positive:

3. Negative: We cannot accept applications by mail. You must come by our office and fill out the proper forms.
   Positive:

4. Negative: We do not deliver on Sunday.
   Positive:

5. Negative: If we can help, don't hesitate to call us.
   Positive:

6. Negative: You won't be sorry you did this.
   Positive:

7. Negative: Thank you for your trouble.
   Positive:

8. Negative: We cannot fill an order that large.
   Positive:

9. Negative: Our tellers are not available after 3 p.m.
   Positive:

10. Negative: This health plan will not cost employees any money.
    Positive:

(proposed solution on pages 194-195)

Exercise 25

Change *passive* voice to *active*:

1. The race car was driven by Smith.

2. The budget was approved by the board.

3. This program has been endorsed by the board of directors.

4. The engines have been rebuilt by outside mechanics.

5. The figures were drawn accurately by the artist.

6. The money was collected by the donation committee.

7. A full report of the incident will be prepared by Kate.

8. It is desired by every faculty member.

9. Your estimates will be checked by the budget department.

10. The Little League game was umpired by John and Susie's dad.

(proposed solution on page 195)

Exercise 26

Rewrite this actual memo.

Vending machines are located near work areas for the convenience of our employees. However, it is necessary to reduce non-productive time to a minimum. I am asking for the cooperation of all employees in voluntarily restraining from using these machines at the following times:

For one hour prior to the beginning of their shifts and for one hour prior to the end of their shifts.

For 30 minutes prior to and following lunch periods and rest breaks as applicable.

Employees must not abuse the use of vending machines. They should, for example, return to their work areas immediately after making their purchases and not loiter or gather in vending machine areas.

Supervision in each department should call any abuse of this privilege to the individual for attention.

_____
_____
_____
_____
_____
_____
_____
_____
_____
_____
_____
_____
_____
_____
_____
_____
_____
_____
_____
_____

(proposed solution on page 196)

Exercise 27

Following is a letter written by a man with more than 10 years of experience in the legal field. He has extensive experience in helping law firms determine how much profit or loss each of their attorneys made. He can help law firms improve their cash flow. He can help law firms put together accurate, concise management reports and he can tell law firms if hiring extra people will help their profit margins. Plus, he can tell law firms how they compare to other law firms when it comes to support staff. Amazingly when he wrote a letter to law firms offering his many talents, he didn't mention any of his services. Instead he wrote this letter:

Dear Mr. Apple:

After 10 years at Jones & Smith, I've decided to try my hand on the "other side" of the business. In that regard, I've joined forces with Roger Hanawalt, the founder and president of Pullem Inc., as vice president/general manager and principal.

Pullem serves law firms and law firms only. Its core business is providing facilities management services (copying, facsimile, mail/messenger, etc.) In addition to providing facilities management services, however, Pullem also provides consulting services. Several of our clients include the biggest law firms on the east coast. Our consulting engagements are performed with the guarantee that if you are not 100 percent satisfied, you owe nothing and are principally in the areas of:

• Automated Systems Services and Network Integration
• Technical Support
• Financial Management
• Operational Reviews
• Marketing Database Design
• Budgeting/Forecasting
• Executive Recruitment

It is in these last several areas where I feel that I offer a particularly unique set of skills. In addition to my 10 years as Jones & Smith's executive director and chief operating officer, I have 10 years of experience as a CPA and corporate controller.

I will give you a call within the next week or so to see if there are any ways in which we might be of assistance. In the meantime, if you have a more immediate need, please do not hesitate to contact me.

Sincerely,

John Claire

_____
_____
_____
_____
_____
_____
_____
_____
_____
_____
_____
_____
_____
_____
_____
_____
_____
_____
_____
_____
_____
_____
_____
_____
_____
_____
_____
_____
_____
_____
_____
_____

(proposed solution on pages 196-197)

Exercise 28

Following is a list of facts about Acme's new corporate headquarters building. You need to write a short three- to four-paragraph memo to employees about their new corporate headquarters. Select the facts that are most pertinent to employees and include them in your memo.

List of facts about Acme's New Corporate Headquarters (CHQ)

Acme will move to its new corporate headquarters at Two Chandler Center, 300 N. 10th St. on April 1 or in about one month. As the first tenant in the complex, Acme will show its continued support for the viability and future of downtown Tulsa. It will also enable our company to more efficiently office about 1,000 workers, previously housed in six leased or owned buildings in downtown and northeast Tulsa.

Chandler Center will cover eight blocks and will include six office buildings, a hotel, retail shopping, parking decks and a three-acre landscaped plaza.

The new Acme headquarters will occupy all but 3.5 floors of the 20-story, 483,000-square-foot office building. Initially Acme is leasing 360,000 square feet, or 16.5 floors, on floors 1 to 14 and 18 to 20. It has an option on remaining floors 15 to 17 to accommodate future growth and needs. Each floor has approximately 22,000 square feet.

Our new Acme building has many energy-saving features, an off-peak storage cooling system, an energy management system to limit and cycle high-demand equipment, high-efficiency motors, chillers, and fluorescent direct lighting; master control of lighting; heavy exterior wall insulation; dual pane windows and revolving doors in the lobby.

All employees will have their offices packed for them and special vans will carry their office materials to the new building. However, employees will be responsible for unpacking their own materials. If you have any personal objects, you might want to hand-carry them.

The first floor main lobby, which Acme will share with future leased retail space, houses a satellite customer service office, a snack shop and an employment information counter. An employee cafeteria is on the second floor. Fourteen elevators—10 passenger, two parking and two freight—service the building.

A nearby parking deck at 5th and Filmore streets accommodates approximately 1,200 employee and visitor vehicles and will cost employees $30 a month.

Acme signed a long-term lease (20 years with renewal options) at a fixed rate with Chandler Center's owner, the T/C Development Corporation. The base-building lease includes the elevator core and immediate flooring and walls, plus electrical, plumbing and air conditioning and heating services to unimproved square footage on each floor.

Acme used an in-house design team for some of the work, thereby saving an estimated $100,000. The Acme designers also handled other building projects.

The design team selected a unified color scheme for the new corporate headquarters. The pastel tones of camel and dark green provide what is called a "timeless look that will always be in vogue."

All furniture in the corporate headquarters is modular and standardized. It is about 20- to 25-percent cheaper and requires 15 to 20 percent less floor space than conventional office furniture. That means employees will work in cubicles about 20-percent smaller than their current offices.

About 85 percent of the artwork in the building is leased from a local gallery for a total of about $1,800 per month.

_____

_____

_____

_____

_____

_____

_____

_____

_____

_____

_____

_____

_____

_____

_____

_____

_____

_____

_____

_____

_____

_____

_____

(proposed solution on page 197)

Exercise 29

You are moving. So you write a moving company and ask for their help. They send you the following letter:

Dear Mr. Woods:

We have received your letter written on July 9, 1996, and understand that you requested that we send around an estimator who could estimate the cost of moving your furniture and household goods for you. According to our schedule, it is convenient for us to send an estimator to your neighborhood around 10 a.m. on the 20th of July and he will analyze and evaluate your needs. He then will come back to our office and chart an estimate which we can send to you right away, without further delay. Thank you for your patronage.

If this moving company handles furniture the same way it does the English language, we're all in trouble. Write a friendly response that says the same thing in a clearer, more straightforward way.

_____
_____
_____
_____
_____
_____
_____
_____
_____
_____
_____
_____
_____
_____
_____
_____
_____

(proposed solution on page 198)

Exercise 30

Following are some simple instructions for adding antifreeze to your car's radiator. The author, however, has not followed the rules of parallel construction, making the instruction difficult to understand. Take the instructions, put them into a list and, of course, make sure they are parallel.

To add antifreeze to your car's engine, you must do the following things. First, make sure the engine is shut off. The next thing is to make sure that the engine has cooled down. This should involve a wait of about half an hour. The cap on the radiator should be turned counter-clockwise. Then, after taking off the cap, look into the radiator, If it is not half-full with water, one must add water. But don't just add water, add antifreeze. This should be a 50/50 mixture. 100 percent water or 100 percent coolant will not protect against overheating or protect the water from freezing on cold nights. After you have added the water, then go ahead and replace the cap. Make sure it is on very tightly.

(proposed solution on page 198)

Exercise 31

The following sentences or phrases are wordy. How would you revise them?

1. At the intersection of Elm and Grove Streets....

2. Two trucks were in a collision....

3. The committee voted to consider an ordinance that will require regulating the activities of teenagers by imposing a curfew upon them of 11 p.m.

4. Thompson was held by the police on a charge of hit-and-run driving, because he was considered to be the prime suspect in the case.

5. A series of lectures on the college level discussing the European influence on Modern Art will be offered by the Colby City Parks and Recreation Department.

6. The long and short of it is that bank interest rates are likely to keep increasing.

7. When you get right down to it, paying 20-percent interest on a credit card is not the smartest thing to do from a financial viewpoint.

8. As you know, by my way of thinking, we should closely consider reinstating a policy of curfews for high school students.

9. As far as the teacher is concerned, her class is ready for the math test.

10. It behooves me to request that you put your dog inside by 10 p.m. as his barking is the cause of many neighbors not sleeping.

_____
_____
_____
_____
_____
_____
_____
_____
_____
_____
_____
_____
_____
_____

(proposed solution on page 198)

Exercise 32

Your boss wants you to summarize a report she has received on potty training. Here is just the introduction. As you read it, remember that she wants to have this long introduction reduced to a good one-paragraph introduction.

No other subject in early childhood is surrounded by as many practical and psychological concerns as the topic of toilet training. Certainly, during the period it is being contemplated and carried out, nothing else seems to have a higher priority or greater importance. Nevertheless, the entire process can be surprisingly smooth and simple as long as readiness is respected and relaxation is the rule.

The reasons why parents may want to have their child trained immediately are numerous and noteworthy. Pressure from relatives and friends, enrollment requirements for preschool, and simply getting tired of dealing with diapers are just a few common considerations. However, no matter how eager parents may be, their efforts are likely to result in frustration unless they hold off until their child is mature enough to handle the situation.

Furthermore, although "training" is the term typically employed, what really takes place is "education." And the easiest and most effective way to educate young children is to teach them what they want to learn when they want to learn it. No matter how determined and methodical parents may be in pursuing their plans, their efforts are likely to cause difficulties and even be counterproductive unless they wait until their child can be recruited as an equally enthusiastic partner in the process. Consequently, patience is the key to successful toilet training.

(proposed solution on page 198)

Exercise 33

The following is an attempt to explain why good accounting practices are crucial to a small business. But has the writer accomplished his or her purpose? Rewrite the paragraph so that it is understandable.

One of the first axioms of accounting is that a business entity can make money only by selling to the outside world. It cannot increase its capital by trading with itself. It follows that, at best, sound internal relationships between the members of a partnership can do more than furnish a favorable climate for the partner's best efforts. At worst, however, unsound relations between partners can and unfortunately often do upset the whole enterprise and the partners with it. Viewed in this light, the paramount purpose of the partners' accounts is to prevent any such adverse developments. The accounts of the partners are therefore, best regarded as instruments for preserving harmonious internal relationships, thereby releasing the time and energy of the members for advancing the real business purposes of the firm. For that reason, the following article is designed to point out how sound principles of partnership accounting may be applied to avoid some common pitfalls. It highlights certain approaches to trouble prevention and to organizational health.

_____
_____
_____
_____
_____
_____
_____
_____
_____
_____
_____
_____
_____
_____
_____
_____
_____
_____
_____

(proposed solution on page 199)

Exercise 34

Following is a typical paragraph from a government publication. Let's put it in English. Note that the excessive use of the passive voice and the lack of strong verbs make this a very weak paragraph.

Unemployment estimates for States and local areas are key indicators of local economic conditions. These estimates, which are produced by State employment security agencies, are used by State and local governments for planning and budgetary purposes and as determinants of the need for local employment and training services and programs. Local area unemployment estimates are also used to determine the eligibility of an area for benefits in various federal assistance programs.

(proposed solution on page 199)

Exercise 35

Another exercise that proves that any piece of writing can be improved by using strong verbs and by eliminating unnecessary words.

Expanding the skills training that is available to adults is central to efforts to improve productivity. Advocates of training programs link them to work organization and productivity. They argue that American firms provide their workers with less training than do comparable firms in other countries. The consequence of this undertraining is that American firms have greater difficulty in adopting particular industrial techniques, such as statistical quality control, and perhaps more seriously face difficulties making their production systems more flexible. As a result, American firms are often less productive and competitive than their counterparts is, say, Germany or Japan.

(proposed solution on page 199)

Proposed solution to exercise 1

When customers close their Equalizer accounts, they sometimes receive a notice that their power will be shut off. Understandably, this upsets them!

Why does a customer get a disconnect notice? If the customer owes money when the account is closed, the computer tags his account as "past due." Then, a few days later, the computer kicks out a "disconnect notice."

The solution is simple. We have programmed the computer to recognize the difference between the closing of an Equalizer account and a past-due bill. Meanwhile, if you get any irate customers on the line, tell them we're sorry and that we have solved the problem.

Thanks!

Proposed solution to exercise 2

Those *!@*!!s are trying to get permission to use our transmission lines, and we ain't gonna let them! Hey, just kidding. Here's the real solution:

A number of competitors would like access to our transmission lines. That way they can sell their electricity to our customers. Their pretense is that it will broaden competition, give consumers a choice and eventually reduce monthly electric bills. Yet, they're not telling the whole truth. Some customers in our service area may see no benefit at all.

Proposed solution to exercise 3

Today, I want to discuss Global Warming and the many activities taking place to stop it. These activities range from international treaties limiting carbon emissions to strict local regulations. All of these actions will force us to add more pollution controls to our plants and cost our customers money.

Yet, we can take steps to stop Global Warming which will not cost us or our customers extra money. Today, I am urging you to consider these steps....

This solution does away with platitudes and moves directly to specifics. It's much stronger.

Proposed solution to exercise 4

Remember, your audience is teenagers—try to identify with them in some way. Here's my version:

> Despite the pessimistic outlook of Beavis and Butthead, there is a tomorrow and we must all live in that tomorrow. But in Tomorrow Land, far too many people will be underfed and overcrowded.
>
> In fact, as I discuss overpopulation, famine and the outlook for the future, I hope to convince you to get involved.

Proposed solution to exercise 5

> I've enclosed a catalog which lists the computer training classes we offer. The classes are listed by degree of difficulty. Thus, a computer novice might take the first few classes listed; someone with more experience might take the classes listed in the back of the catalog.
>
> A word of caution: If your employees sign up for a class, please make sure they can work on a computer on a daily basis. We find students don't remember what they learned in class if they can't work on a computer right away.

Proposed solution to exercise 6

> Senior management has identified seven key habits that will make our company successful. If we all adopt these habits, our customers will be satisfied and we can continue to pay bonuses every year. Here are the habits we all must strive to make part of our everyday work life.
>
> 1. Customer driven: We have limited resources. Let's use them in the most effective way possible to keep our customers satisfied. Let's keep working on lowering the cost of our product while increasing our level of customer service. Let's support our front-line people, those folks who meet customers every day. And let's do our best to support each other!

Note that instead of wasting all that space trying to convince employees of how important these characteristics are, I tied them to something they understand. Most people want good habits, not bad habits. And everyone knows that good habits make you healthier, just as they can make a company healthier. Employees will probably be familiar with this use of the word "habits" if they have heard of the book *Seven Habits of Highly Successful People*.

Proposed solution to exercise 7

Dear Speaker of the House:

More people are dying on the highways of Arkansas than anywhere else. We have increased the speed limit on rural roads and that has increased the number of people dying in car crashes by 58 percent. Every eight minutes someone in Arkansas is hurt in a car wreck.

And while the legislature talks, deaths increase. It is time to take action, time to end this senseless slaughter of Arkansas citizens. Pass the mandatory seat belt law now!

Will the citizens of Arkansas support such a bill? Yes. They're tired of having the most dangerous place in Arkansas be the inside of a car.

In short, the time for talking has passed. Too many citizens have been injured just because they weren't belted up. Let's pass a seat belt law. Now!

Very truly yours,

P.S. The nation's first seat belt law, in New York, increased the use of seat belts in 1985 from 16 to 60 percent, saving 1,300 lives and preventing or reducing about 90,000 injuries.

Note that the information on the New York seat belt law was not in the original draft. But a little research can add impact to your letter. Also, remember that the most read part of a letter, after the heading, is the postscript.

Proposed solution to exercise 8

The Key Accounts Program means we call our biggest and best customers on a regular basis to ensure we are providing the best service possible.

Proposed solution to exercise 9

Steve said if his marketing group comes up with a great marketing program that will help one of our customers, he will talk to the account representative. The account representative can then offer the program to his or her customer.

Proposed solution to exercise 10

Throw the thing out and start over. Here's a rewrite.

Before you buy that new home, read this. It can save you more than $1,000.

That's right, buying a Total-electric Home can save you more than $1,000. These savings add up year after year. *That's extra money you can put toward your mortgage instead of utility bills.*

- $1,000 saved because you didn't have to hook up gas fixtures.
- $150 a year saved through the use of a high-efficiency heat pump.
- $30 a year saved by eliminating "leaks."
- $45 a year saved with great insulation.
- $80 a year saved by sun screens. They also protect and preserve your carpet.

Total up these savings and they point to one thing: the Total-electric Home. Call me and I'll help you start putting that money in the bank. Unless, of course, you want to keep sending it to your utility company.

For savings right now, call 555-3456.

Proposed solution to exercise 11

Please read this carefully. It will determine how much money you can save for your retirement.

The company has decided to increase its "match" of the money in your 401K plan. Before, we matched five percent of your paycheck. We will now match up to six percent.

To get the six percent match, simply fill out a new form. Contact Employee Benefits to request a Change Form.

NOTE: If you are already putting six percent or more of your paycheck into your 401K, you don't need to fill out a new form. The change to six percent will be automatically taken care of by that mysterious computer at Corporate Headquarters.

Proposed solution to exercise 12

To: All Employees
Subject: Long Distance Call Change

Dear Employee:
On March 10, we will switch over to a new long-distance system. This means that you will be assigned a new 10-digit code you must dial before you can make a call. Don't worry; it won't be that tough. The code can be programmed into your phone, so you only have to push one button.

You'll receive your new long-distance code in about two weeks with clear directions on how to use it.

Thanks!

I'll admit, I sandbagged you a bit with this memo. But its audience is employees, who only want to know what numbers to push to make a phone call. They don't care about the technical details of the system, only the engineer writing the memo does. He obviously did not think about his audience before writing the memo. Remember, when writing a memo, think, "What does my audience need to know? What do they want to know?" Then give them the information they need and want, not the information you want to give to impress them.

Proposed solution to exercise 13

You may be laying off a lot of people. That's traumatic, especially if your company has always bragged about job security and employee loyalty. Realignment lets you use this traumatic period to get rid of the old ideas and work habits and instill new ones in your company.

But realignment requires attention to detail. A series of steps, all of them crucial, must be carried out at the right time and place. You can't simply take a step here and a step there. A coordinated plan must state when each step will occur.

Also, you must guarantee that each program will work. We have seen one company brag about its internal placement program. After it was launched, the company realized it had no jobs to give employees. The effect was like a neutron bomb on employee morale.

Another major hurdle to overcome is the employees' distrust. Employees have seen management programs come and go. What makes realignment different? To convince employees, you must be out there, in the trenches, talking to them and convincing them that realignment is crucial if the company is to survive.

Proposed solution to exercise 14

We're trying to reduce our air conditioning and heating costs. We have installed a new heating/cooling system which will operate from 8 a.m. to 6 p.m. Monday through Saturday.

After 6 p.m., it will automatically shut off. If you have to come into work after hours or on Sunday and you don't want to freeze or sweat to death, call Property Services. They will turn on the air conditioning for you.

Remember, if you want air conditioning or heating after hours, you must call Property Services.

Thanks!

Proposed solution to exercise 15

We have had a serious accident that could have been avoided. A worker's toe was crushed, and he may lose it. Following simple safety procedures could have stopped this accident.

When a line crew was putting away a boom, the driver started to raise the truck's stiff legs. Because a worker was on the left back side of the truck, the driver raised the right stiff legs first.

This caused weight to shift, and the worker's foot was crushed by the shifting left stiff leg.

The solution is very simple. Before raising any stiff leg, make sure no one is near the truck. When the outriggers are moved, make sure no one is around them.

If someone is near the truck, do not raise any stiff legs!

Proposed solution to exercise 16

Jo Lou, president, announced Friday the Phoenix Neighborhood Alliance will hold a protest demanding the city demolish a rat-infested house where children play.

Proposed solution to exercise 17

Our employee survey highlighted an alarming trend that we must stop. Unless we act quickly, our efforts toward an employee-driven culture will be blocked.

The employee survey showed we don't understand the concerns of our employees! This is a serious accusation. Only by understanding the needs of our employees can we empower them to do their best work. Therefore, as a major step towards better understanding our employees, we will host a crucial focus group.

You have been selected to be a member of this crucial group, and your first task is to study the attached questionnaire. It lists the areas that employees were most upset about and the areas in which we must improve.

Unfortunately, the employees gave only vague responses, such as, "There is too much favoritism." To enable supervisors to better understand employees' concerns, we must develop concrete examples.

For instance, instead of "favoritism," we might say, "Supervisors don't count absenteeism for some employees; they promote their 'buddies,' " etc.

After four hours, we will have a list of specific examples; we can then better educate our supervisors on exactly what employees are talking about.

I'm looking forward to seeing you on _____.

Proposed solution to exercise 18

Sarwark Motors, founded in 1942, claims the distinction of being the oldest continually operated used car dealership in the state of Arizona. It was started by my father, Roman Sarwark, who came to Arizona from Indiana after almost dying of tuberculosis.

After heeding the advice of his doctors to live in a warm climate, Roman established Sarwark Motors at the corner of 16th Street and Van Buren, where it still stands today. But while the location hasn't changed, the name has. It is now known as Consolidated Auto Sales.

Back then, Van Buren was comparable to the Bell road of today. Most new car dealers were clustered around Central and Van Buren; over the years, they slowly migrated north, but we stayed.

For a while, in the 50s and 60s, my father tried his hand at new car franchises, including a Volvo dealership, and he also ran a used car lot on Camelback, at the current site of ABC Nissan.

Always one to experiment, my father also ventured into the mobile home business. The business did well during the 60s and 70s; in fact, in 1971 we sold more than 300 mobile homes, quite an accomplishment. However, in 1980 my father decided to discontinue the mobile home business and return to what he knew and loved bast, the car business.

From almost the beginning of his career, my father discovered the value of carrying contracts for his customers, or as it is known, the "Buy-Here-Pay-Here" business. He knew that he had good customers, but due to their financial conditions, they couldn't get bank financing.

I can remember looking at records and seeing deals in which the car sold for $995, with $50 down and $15 weekly payments. Through the years, inflation has taken its toll; most of our cars now sell for more than $4,000.

But our customers, despite inflation and changing times, have stayed loyal. We have many customers whose parents first bought cars from my father many years ago. They like the casual family atmosphere; a permanent feature at our cashier's window is a jar of candies available for anyone. We also have toys we give to the children of our customers.

I also liked the family atmosphere; in fact, I liked it so much, I started working for my father in 1972 and literally learned the business from the ground up. As the years progressed, I gradually assumed more and more of the duties that my father had performed.

Roman is now 82, and he has decided it's time I take over as president of our family business, Consolidated Motors. But Roman is too valuable to us, so we won't let him retire. He will remain as an active advisor but will play less of a role in the day-to-day operations of our company.

I realize I have a big responsibility. I must fill the position my father has held for so many years. I must continue the business he spent his life building, and I must work hard to ensure its continued success.

It won't be easy; it will be a challenge, but one I look forward to. Like every car dealership, we must continually evaluate our strategies in the light of today's evolving business climate.

This is a crucial time in the used car business; the competition is stronger than I have ever seen it. But these challenges will be changed into opportunities which will allow Consolidated Auto Sales to thrive for another 50 years.

Proposed solution to exercise 19

Yes, we have reorganized the Human Resource Department! But we are still dedicated to affirmative action and equal employment opportunities. In fact, our newly appointed Employee Relations Representative will act as the full-service focal point for all affirmative action and equal employment opportunity concerns.

When is a good time to call us? If you (or your supervisor) have any employment problem you can't solve, including those relating to equal employment opportunities, please call us.

Proposed solution to exercise 20

More than 300 participants jammed the Holiday Inn in San Diego too discuss expanding composting and recycling programs. Speakers, from a variety of agendas, ranging from private institutions to government bureaus, gave exhilirating lectures on topics ranging from faculty management to economic opportunities. An open forum on "Increasing the Role of Composting on the West Coast" gave everyone a chance to express their views and to question a panel of experts.

Proposed solution to exercise 21

Where is the long-awaited recovery? Well, it's a quiet recovery. Housing permits are up significantly, as are retail sales. But these increases haven't made a lot of noise. They have not translated into strong growth in either the wage or salary sector. In fact, expectations have declined and ourr panel sees a matching decline in employement and personal income. Quite frankly, the government, consumers and businesses are carrying too much debt and no one is eager to rush out and buy anything. Especially when low inflation means that you won't get a big pay raise next year.

Proposed solution to exercise 22

The person hired will:

- Be responsible for the work done by housekeeping staff.
- Post work schedules.
- Document all training.
- Help orient new employees.
- Decide what work must be done and who will do it.
- Be responsible for correcting problems.
- Be responsible for determining sick leave, AWOL and other employee-related concerns.

Proposed solution to exercise 23

Nearly everyone agrees that the welfare system should train people for jobs. Yet as congress and state legislature consider welfare reform, they must consider how tough it is for AFDC mothers to find a decent, well-paying job. Many AFDC mothers have low skills, have no work experience and have not even graduated from high school.

Proposed solution to exercise 24

1. Negative: Because you failed to say what size shirt you wear, we cannot send it.
   Positive: Please send us your correct shirt size and we'll send it promptly.

2. Negative: We're sorry we cannot offer you television spots for $1,000.
   Positive: We're pleased that we can offer you television spots for just $1,100.

3. Negative: We cannot accept applications by mail. You must come by our office and fill out the proper forms.
   Positive: We are pleased to have you apply. Please come by our office and fill out the proper forms.

4. Negative: We do not deliver on Sunday.
   Positive: We are pleased to deliver six days a week—Monday through Saturday.

5. Negative: If we can help, don't hesitate to call us.
   Positive: Please call us if you need assistance.

6. Negative: You won't be sorry you did this.
   Positive: You'll be glad you did this.

7. Negative: Thank you for your trouble.
   Positive: Thank you for taking the time to call us.

8. Negative: We cannot fill an order that large.
   Positive: We would be pleased to fill your order in two shipments.

9. Negative: Our tellers are not available after 3 p.m.
   Positive: After 3 p.m., please feel free to use our state-of-the-art banking machines.

10. Negative: This health plan will not cost employees any money.
    Positive: This health plan is free to employees.

Proposed solution to exercise 25

1. The race car was driven by Smith.
   Smith drove the race car.

2. The budget was approved by the board.
   The board approved the budget.

3. This program has been endorsed by the board of directors.
   The board of directors endorsed this program.

4. The engines have been rebuilt by outside mechanics.
   Outside mechanics rebuilt the engines.

5. The figures were drawn accurately by the artist.
   The artist drew the figures accurately.

6. The money was collected by the donation committee.
   The donation committee collected the money.

7. A full report of the incident will be prepared by Kate.
   Kate will prepare a full report of the incident.

8. It is desired by every faculty member.
   Every member desires it.

9. Your estimates will be checked by the budget department.
   The budget department will check your estimates.

10. The soccer team was coached by John and Susie's dad.
    John and Susie's dad coached the soccer team.

Proposed solution to exercise 26

We have placed vending machines near your work area for your convenience. To help us all be more productive, could we all try to avoid using the machines an hour before we work and an hour before we quit? Also, it would be very helpful if we could avoid using the machines 30 minutes before or after lunch breaks.

Thanks for your help! If we all get to work as soon as possible after using the machines, we can increase our productivity. Once again, thanks for your cooperation and teamwork.

Proposed solution to exercise 27

Please note that before you write your own version, that John Claire was selling both his company's services and his own services. That's just too much to sell in one letter. Concentrate on one area. Also, notice that John didn't give any specific details of how he can exactly help the client. Instead he gave a list of vague terms. Exactly what did John mean by "Operation Reviews"? What did he mean by "Financial Management"? Also notice John really didn't answer the "What's in it for me?" question. He needs to tell the client exactly how he can help save money, be more organized, make more of a profit, and so forth. Finally, John *does* have a lot to offer and we covered that in the first paragraph. Now, knowing all of this, here is the proposed solution:

Dear Mr. Apple:

With more than 10 years of experience as the chief operating officer for one of the Southwest's most successful law firms, I know exactly where law firms make money and where they lose money. I know the basic strategic mistakes they make and how they can enhance their revenue with very little effort.

My law experience, combined with 10 additional years practicing as a CPA and corporate controller, gives me an excellent basis for helping you answer the following questions:

- How much profit (or loss?) did each of our attorneys and paralegals generate for our firm last year?
- How can our income statement indicate that we're making a profit, but the cash isn't available to distribute to our partners?
- Why can't I receive accurate, concise management reports, telling me what I need to know about each timekeeper as well as the firm in its entirety, on a timely basis?
- What will the effect on our firm's profitability be if we add x number of associates? What about the effect on cash flow?
- Is the size and compensation of our support staff comparable to other similarly sized firms?

I'd like to put my expertise to work for you and help you find the answers to these types of questions. As I'm very sensitive to the busy schedules of attorneys, I merely ask for 15 minutes of your time to show you a specific study I have completed for another law firm. You'll see how I was able to identify specific problems and make specific recommendations.

As I'm very sensitive to the busy schedule of attorneys, I merely ask for 15 minutes of your time to show you a specific study I have completed for another law firm. You'll see how I was able to identify specific problems and make specific recommendations.

I will call you within the next week to schedule a mutually convenient time for us to meet.

Proposed solution to exercise 28

Now, remember, when writing this memo, you have a lot of information to put into four paragraphs. Choose the information that you think will interest your reader. Forget the other stuff!

To all employees:

Good news! We will be moving to our new offices on April 1. Even more good news is that you don't have to pack up your offices. A professional moving company will do it for you and then put the boxes in your new office. You will have to unpack them yourselves. A word of caution: If you have any personal items, like favorite family photos in your office, I would suggest that you carry those over yourself.

One advantage to the move is that we will all finally be in the same building. We don't have to run all over town visiting our separate offices. Another advantage is that we will have more parking space. The high-rise garage will hold all our cars. Parking will cost each employee $30 a month.

People have been worried that they might have a smaller office. Yes, your cubicles will be about 20-percent smaller than the offices you have now. But you may not notice the decrease in space, because the new modular furniture takes up less space than our old, heavy wood furniture.

Finally—and I know this has been a major question—yes, there is a snack shop so we can still escape and eat our favorite snacks. There will also be a great cafeteria on the second floor.

I'll keep you posted as we receive more information about the new building.

Proposed solution to exercise 29

Dear Mr. Woods:

Thank you for considering our moving company. We can have a representative out to your house on July 20. After seeing what needs to be moved, he can give you an accurate estimate by July 22. We are looking forward to helping you move!

Proposed solution to exercise 30

To add antifreeze to your car's engine, do the following:

- Make sure the engine is shut off.
- Wait one half-hour so the engine can cool.
- Untwist the cap (counter-clockwise).
- If the radiator is half-empty, add 50 percent coolant and 50 percent water.
- Replace the cap. Ensure it is tight.

Proposed solution to exercise 31

1. At Elm and Grove....
2. Two trucks collided....
3. The committee will consider an 11 p.m. curfew for teenagers.
4. The police held Thompson on a charge of hit-and-run driving.
5. Colby's Parks and Recreation Department will hold a series of college lectures on the European Influence on Modern Art.
6. Bank interest rates will keep rising.
7. Paying 20-percent interest on a credit card is not smart.
8. We should have curfews for teenagers.
9. The teacher thinks her class is ready for the test.
10. Please put your dog in at 10 p.m. His barking keeps the whole neighborhood awake.

Proposed solution to exercise 32

For a variety of reasons, including you're sick of dirty diapers, you may want to potty train your child. But your time schedule and his are not the same. He will not be potty-trained until he is ready. So keep putting up with the dirty diapers, don't push the child (this will only be frustrating) and practice patience. When the child is ready to learn, it will be easier on both of you.

Proposed solution to exercise 33

You cannot make money unless you sell something. To make money, you must have faith in your partners and avoid internal bickering. That way, you can concentrate on your real business, selling to customers. The best way to maintain faith in your partners? Have a good accounting system that everyone understands, so everyone knows how the money is being spent. The following article highlights the best way to set up fair accounting systems.

Proposed solution to exercise 34

State and local governments depend upon unemployment estimates to draft plans and to make budgets. The estimates help to determine the need for local employment services, including training services and programs. Local unemployment estimates also qualify an area for various federal assistance programs.

Proposed solution to exercise 35

Training programs improve organizational skills and productivity. To improve productivity, we must offer adults more skills training. Unfortunately, because American firms provide workers with less training than foreign firms, they face difficulties in adopting industrial techniques, such as statistical quality control. Plus, they have trouble improving the flexibility of their production systems. This means American firms are less productive than counterparts in Germany or Japan.

Index